D1298595

# REBELS AND UNDERDOGS

# REBELS AND UNDERDOGS

## THE STORY OF OHIO ROCK AND ROLL

## GARIN PIRNIA

**RED ⚡ LIGHTNING BOOKS**

*This book is a publication of*

Red Lightning Books

1320 East 10th Street

Bloomington,

Indiana 47405

USA

redlightningbooks.com

© 2018 by Garin Pirnia

All rights reserved

No part of this book may be
reproduced or utilized in any form or
by any means, electronic or mechanical,
including photocopying and recording,
or by any information storage and
retrieval system, without
permission in writing from
the publisher. The Association of
American University Presses' Resolution on
Permissions constitutes the only exception to this
prohibition. The paper used in this publication meets
the minimum requirements of the American National
Standard for Information Sciences—Permanence of Paper
for Printed Library Materials, ANSI Z39.48–1992.

Manufactured in the United States of America

ISBN 978-1-68435-011-7 (cloth)
ISBN 978-1-68435-012-4 (paperback)
ISBN 978-1-68435-015-5 (ebook)

1  2  3  4  5   23  22  21  20  19  18

TO THE ROCK AND ROLL WEIRDOS:

KEEP KEEPING IT WEIRD.

# Contents

# Introduction

OHIO IS A WEIRD STATE. IT'S AN EVEN WEIRDER PLACE TO grow up. With Lake Erie to the north and the Ohio River to the south, Ohio is otherwise landlocked. Winters are harsh, and summers are uncomfortably hot and humid. The seasons make it rife for Ohioans to spend a lot of time indoors, in basements and garages, drubbing on instruments and creating art. The idea for this book germinated from my realizing just how many amazing musicians have formed bands or were born in the Buckeye State. When we think of music scenes, we think of New York City, Los Angeles, Chicago, Seattle, Nashville, and Austin—but an entire state dedicated to one great band after the next? And they each sound different and have their own individualities? How is that possible? So I dug deep and interviewed more than thirty folks associated with the rock and roll scene in their Ohio hometowns (and a few who didn't grow up in Ohio). The one question I asked everybody was, *What was it about Ohio that bred these bands?* Was there something specific to Ohio? The consensus seemed to be that a lot of bands formed out of boredom or to combat their working-class environs. Ohioans had both an underdog and rebellious attitude in that they were going to carve their own paths, no matter what. "I think there's humility and a certain understanding of sadness in Ohio, especially among creative people," Jerry Casale, the cofounder of Devo, says. "They're not competing with each other and hating each other like in big cities. Frankly, nobody was paying attention to any of us, so it isn't like you're sucking up to the local press or thinking someone from a TV station is coming down with somebody from a record company and you got to blow this other band away, and all those things that happen in the big city. In Ohio, nobody gave a shit."

I also asked everyone what the rock scene was like in their cities and how it changed over the years. I wasn't interested in writing a book that regurgitated history you could read in another book or on Wikipedia. I was interested in the socioeconomic factors that comprised those scenes. I was fascinated by how some bands metamorphosed from "local band" to "global sensation" while other outfits slaved away and went nowhere. The 1990s and the 2000s were transformative eras for bands, divided into pre- and post-internet. With the advent of online streaming services and Napster, the music industry almost imploded. People don't buy albums like they did twenty years ago. In some ways it's harder to start a band today than decades ago—yet bands still succeed.

My musical journey also began out of boredom. I grew up in Centerville, a suburb of Dayton. In the nineties I listened to the radio and watched MTV to discover new music. I was aware of the Dayton band the Breeders, but I don't think I was cognizant that they manufactured their craft in my hometown. I attended Ohio University in Athens for three years and then moved to Los Angeles to pursue a film career. In 2002 Amoeba Records opened in Hollywood, and I went there at least twice a week to listen to and buy CDs. I got into music more, and I realized I had a voice in writing. At the end of 2003 I moved back to Dayton and worked mundane jobs. The office drudgery had one silver lining: I was able to stream radio stations and listen to CDs. WOXY (known as 97X) was a radio station once based in Oxford, Ohio. Listening to modern rock propelled me to start my career as a music journalist. In January 2004 I published my first-ever album review, on a Canadian-based website called *Coke Machine Glow*. A few months later I moved to Chicago and began writing (for free) for *Chicago Innerview* magazine, a local zine that featured interviews with bands coming to town. From there I spent the next seven years bolstering my resume by interviewing hundreds of bands (mostly national and international groups) and attending scores of concerts and music fests (such as Lollapalooza and the Pitchfork Festival), and I eventually got paid for my work. I met like-minded people who were audiophiles and liked to spend evenings at rock clubs. There were occasions when I attended two shows in one night. There were times when I went to four nights of shows in a row. I couldn't keep up that kind of pace today. In 2011 I said goodbye to Chicago's fecund rock scene and moved closer to home, to Covington, Kentucky, near Cincinnati. I continued to write about local music, but this time I got to meet some of my hometown heroes: Robert "Bob" Pollard, Matt Berninger, and Kelley Deal. They, along with three of the four members of the boy band 98 Degrees, were accessible. They were Ohio nice. In writing this book I had the opportunity to befriend some rock stars I grew up listening to on the radio, such as Happy Chichester of Howlin' Maggie and Richard Patrick of Filter.

With that said, *Rebels and Underdogs* isn't the definitive history of Ohio music—that would work better as a tome. Even though one of the foundations for Ohio rock and roll music was funk, and many of the people I interviewed said the music and the artists influenced them, I decided to exclude both funk and R&B, as I think those genres are so big in Ohio that they deserve their own stand-alone books. (This is by no means me trying to bury a mostly black form of music; funk artists get some due in the book.) I reached out to more people than those included in the book, but some of them either declined to participate or ignored my requests.

This is a book about my musical history, but, more importantly, it's a book about my home state and the rock and roll stories that came from it—and keep coming. It's a tapestry of stories told from troubadours who not only were on the scene but also made the scene. It's weighted in life and death. Several of these bands changed the face of rock and roll, both in Ohio and throughout the world. Where would our culture be without Devo? Bob Pollard's poetic lyrics? Or the industrial sound of Nine Inch Nails? What if punk hadn't existed in Cleveland as it did? *Rebels and Underdogs* is the stuff rock and roll dreams are made of—and most of these dreams came true.

# Acknowledgments

TO ADAM, FOR ATTENDING COUNTLESS CONCERTS AND MUSIC festivals with me, and for willingly spending time in Northeast Ohio with me.

To Diablo, for being my alarm clock (whether I liked it or not), and for stealing my desk chair and letting me know it was time to stop working for the day (so he could sleep).

To my family, who grew up in Ohio—my mom and her family in Akron, Dawn near Cleveland, my brothers and other cousins in Dayton, Blake in Columbus—they're true Ohioans.

To the rock stars from Ohio who didn't live long enough—we will remember you.

To Chuck Berry, for laying down the foundation for rock and roll.

To *Chicago Innerview* magazine, for giving me my first big journalism gig.

To Cleveland's Rock and Roll Hall of Fame Library and Archives, for allowing me to spend a day perusing their Jane Scott and Northeast Ohio Sound collections.

To all of the editors who let me write about music.

To the bands' and artists' publicists and managers, for facilitating interviews.

To everybody I talked to for the book—thank you for being generous with your time, and thank you for sharing your life stories with me.

To Ashley Runyon of Indiana University Press, for taking a chance on me twice, and for letting me write this book. And to everybody else who worked on the book with me.

To nitro coffee, for giving me the caffeine fix I needed.

To my hometown of Dayton, for shaping who I am.

To my mom's hometown of Akron, for instilling in her a strong work ethic, which trickled down to me.

To Steve, for introducing me to Guided by Voices and so many other great Ohio and non-Ohio bands.

To the photographers who captured the Ohio music scene throughout the past several decades—they're the true warriors.

To Fiona the Hippo, for being a cute distraction.

To Mark and Julie, for twenty-plus years of friendship and support.

To the "Akron Sound" Museum, for archiving Akron's rock music history.

# REBELS AND UNDERDOGS

# 1

# AKRON/KENT

NO OTHER OHIO METROPOLIS REPRESENTS THE UNDERDOG ethos more than Akron, aka the Rubber Capital of the World. In 2016 a basketball player from Akron named LeBron James won Cleveland's first sports title in fifty-two years. At the turn of the century, a little band named the Black Keys made Akron's music scene relevant again. Situated twenty-two minutes from Akron, Kent State University shared a lot of the same DNA with the musicians coming from there. Jerry Casale of Devo was born in Kent but settled down in Akron after college. Chris Butler (Tin Huey, the Waitresses, and 15-60-75 the Numbers Band) grew up in Cleveland, attended Kent State, and also landed in Akron. Chrissie Hynde of the Pretenders was another Kent Stater around the same time, in the early 1970s. The Akron music venue the Crypt was a showcase for local bands like the Bizarros, Devo, Unit 5, Hammer Damage, and the Rubber City Rebels, and is considered one of the first punk clubs to operate outside of New York City. Akron had pop music, too, with Akron native Rachel Sweet and Rex Smith's hit 1981 song, "Everlasting Love." It's worth noting that Marilyn Manson, Jani Lane of eighties hair metal band Warrant, and Lux Interior of the punk group the Cramps

were born in the Akron-Canton region but didn't form their alter
egos until they moved away from the state.

The "Akron Sound," as it came to be known, encompassed bands
forming and playing gigs in the 1970s through the mid-1980s. In
1982 the rubber tire industry took a final gasp and died, and in 1984
Walter Mondale and the media coined the term "Rust Belt." So what
else was there to do other than start a band? "A lot came out of here,
whether it was a desire to get the hell out or a raging desire to matter,"
Butler says. In 1978 Mark Mothersbaugh of Devo was in Liverpool,
England. A reporter asked him what Akron was like, and he said,
"Actually, it's a lot like Liverpool," meaning Akron was downtrodden
and working class. But the reporter misunderstood his response and
assumed Rubber City had a music scene like Liverpool, that Akron
was prepping the next Beatles. Robert Christgau of the *Village Voice*
visited Akron and wrote a long feature, published in April 1978.[1] Because of the article's scope, many bands got signed to major labels,
but some, like Chi-Pig, were left behind. The city's sound has been
immortalized in two PBS documentaries—*It's Everything, and Then
It's Gone* and *If You're Not Dead, Play*—and in the "Akron Sound"
Museum.[2] Museum founder Wayne Beck acquired hundreds of posters, flyers, newspaper clippings, photos, and even a Devo Energy
Dome to display the ephemera in a public brick-and-mortar location.

While coming of age in Cleveland in the 1960s, Butler noticed
how difficult it was for a local band to break out. He describes the
"holy triumvirate": monopolizing bookers Jules and Mike Belkin,
WMMS radio, and the Northeast Ohio publication *Scene*. "You had
this big rock and roll market," he says. "You had a big audience that
wanted to go out and see live music, and you had these gatekeepers
who were very reluctant. If you were in any kind of band that was
creative, you got closed out. That gave you—definitely in the scene
that I was in—a sense of 'what about me?' and a real drive to get
known. If they wouldn't let you in, then we were the classic definition of DIY." In the music world the term "DIY," or "Do It Yourself,"
means building your brand independently, from the ground up,

using self-promotion and handmade items as tools. Butler says bands had to find their own recording equipment and start their own zines to gain traction.

Between Kent, Cleveland, and Akron, bands shared gigs. "It's like anything—the freaks come out at night," Jerry Casale says. "Creative people tended to glom onto the other creative people because it was a small pool, so you all knew each other and were supportive of each other. It was fantastic. It was a hard time. This was when Northeast Ohio was crumbling. The economy was terrible and nobody had anything, so what else was there to do but create."

Akronite Chuck Auerbach, father of Black Keys guitar player and vocalist Dan Auerbach, is an antiques dealer and has an inkling as to why so many bands sprouted from the region. "The thing that is interesting about Ohio is that it was a perfect mix of it being settled very early on in the late eighteenth century . . . so it was rural and agricultural for most of its time. And then it became industrial and modern. For me as an antiques dealer, there's a great mix of country and modern, and I think it also shows up in the music. There's traditional and then there is contemporary. California—I'm not sure if you can say that about its music."

Jeri Sapronetti of the Akron group Time Cat—which formed in 2011—grew up in Akron and says her hometown could use more music venues. "There's a couple hundred people in Akron who are devoted to the arts and music, so there is a lot going on," she says. "But a lot of it is jazz and soul, and not a lot of rock and roll. There's one venue we really need that doesn't exist yet."

In 2010 Akron's population dipped to less than two hundred thousand, the lowest since the 1920 census. However, the metro area is not as depressed as it was in the 1960s–1980s. Goodyear Tire and Rubber Company, the polymer industry, and the University of Akron keep the city afloat. The struggle gets reflected in the music, too. "I feel like we have the underdog thing going on," Sapronetti says. "I think that comes out in the music. People want to try harder when you're fighting against these odds, so there's an underdog quality and a weirdo quality. There's definitely a thing people in Akron have that I can't identify. It's hard to put my finger on what that sound is. It's a weird struggle, but when you believe in yourself and you believe in music, then you'll believe in somehow you'll manage to escape this."

"I think the true authentic rock and rollers, or musicians in general, are the outsiders," says David Giffels, University of Akron academic and author of the books *We Are DEVO!* and *The Hard Way on Purpose*.[3] "I think that's essential: the weirdos, the outcasts, the ones who want it more. The star quarterback is never going to be the great front man—the great front man is the kid who got beat up by the star quarterback." Giffels has lived in Akron his whole life and knows he devoted his life to something special. "To have that great Cavs victory and great shedding of that long period of hardship done by somebody who says, 'I'm just a kid from Akron'—there's a pride here."

### THE BLACK KEYS

*I think the Black Keys will be regarded as the last American band to just start a band, to get a van and start from the bottom.*

—David Giffels

Dan Auerbach and Patrick Carney, the blues-rock-guitar-drums powerhouse duo from Akron known as the Black Keys, have been referred to as the saviors of rock and as the last great rock band of the pre-internet age. But here's a fact: they've been one of the most prosperous bands to emerge from Ohio and the biggest band to come from Akron since the mid-1980s.

It all started when Auerbach—who was born in Athens, Ohio— was coming of age in Akron. "Dan didn't want to start a band necessarily," Chuck Auerbach says. "He wanted to play music. We had spent a lot of time with his mom's family, all of whom are musicians. They play bluegrass, and every time the family would get together they would all play music. And Dan really enjoyed the music and always wanted to join in. So that was some of the inspiration for him wanting to play music." Dan's cousin was guitarist Robert Quine, who played with luminaries like Richard Hell and Lou Reed. In 1996, now a teenager, Dan started playing music with his schoolmate Patrick Carney. (Pat's uncle is Ralph Carney, Tin Huey's saxophonist.) In 2001 Carney helped Auerbach record a demo to send to labels, and soon after they started playing gigs at downtown Akron's Lime Spider. They took some courses at the University of Akron but dropped out to pursue music full-time, something Chuck supported. "My wife and I encouraged him to do that," Auerbach says. "It's turned out pretty well. If you're lucky enough to have a kid who knows what he loves and is willing to work very hard and pursue that, then you should back them up." Chuck is like a cheerleader—he doles out advice in the most positive way. No wonder Dan—and his brother, Geoff, a social worker—turned out to be so winning. "Both of my kids found out what they really want to do and are working hard to get it done," Auerbach says.

Though it may seem like the Black Keys had a swift growth, it took years of hard work for them to have a hit. In 2002 they released *The Big Come Up* on Alive Records. Then they signed to the Mississippi-based Fat Possum Records and released *Thickfreakness*. Next came *Rubber Factory* the following year and *Magic Potion* in 2006—their first major label release, on Nonesuch, a subsidiary of Warner Bros. Finally, in 2008, they had their first gold record with *Attack and Release*, which peaked at number fourteen on the US charts. *Brothers*, in 2010, was their breakout record. It hit number three on the charts, went platinum, and in 2011 it won Carney and Auerbach three Grammy Awards, including Best Alternative Music Album. Michael Carney, Pat's brother, won a Grammy for Best Recording Package for the minimal album cover that simply read, "This is an album by The Black Keys. The name of this album is Brothers." in white and red lettering on black. The 2011 pre-awards ceremony wasn't broadcast live on TV, but in 2013 the Black Keys returned to the Grammys nominated for their 2011 release *El Camino* and this time not only did they accept one award on live TV—Best Rock Performance was presented to them by the Ohio-born Dave Grohl, of both Nirvana and Foo Fighters fame—but they also played their award-winning song "Lonely Boy" during the broadcast. *El Camino* sold 1.4 million copies. The duo cut the record *True Blue*—a reference to a catchphrase the great Ghoulardi from Cleveland used to say—in 2014, and it became their first number one record. (It did not sell as well as *El Camino*, though.) Finding an overwhelming amount of fame, fortune, and success, the guys left Akron in 2011 for Music City, aka Nashville, where Auerbach opened his recording studio, Easy Eye.

"Their music is very real; it's very primal," Chuck Auerbach says about the band's appeal. "Pat's drums kick you right in the gut. Dan is a good guitar player. I think they became really good songwriters. I can't speak for anybody but myself, but when I listen to their music I get the same feeling I had listening to rock and roll of the nineteen fifties and sixties that I grew up with. There is a tradition that gets lost every couple years in music, and I think Pat and Dan reconnected to that tradition."

When Dan was a child, Chuck noticed that his son's musical tastes "were different than any other kid I've ever met who wanted to be a musician," and included bluesmen Robert Johnson, Junior Kimbrough, and R. L. Burnside. Even if you haven't downloaded a Black Keys song or bought one of their records, you've probably heard them blaring on the jukebox at your local bar or heard "Tighten Up" playing over the end credits of a TV show or in a movie trailer. They have licensed their music to about three hundred outlets and through licensing have inevitably reached more people than they would just getting played on the radio. The Black Keys are everywhere—whether you're consciously aware of them or not.

"The Black Keys moved to Nashville, but they still associate strongly with Akron as their home," David Giffels says. "They've always made a point to shout out Akron in public opportunities. They refer to themselves as being from Akron, and that's a pride you'll pick up on. It's significant for Ohio's rock bands to associate being from Ohio, because we've spent the last few decades being anonymous and misunderstood. So when we have these ambassadors like Black Keys, Chrissie Hynde, Chris Butler, and others, it's important culturally for the city to have that association with someone who is known beyond here. It extends to LeBron James, too."

Giffels and NBA championship-winning Cleveland Cavaliers' LeBron "King James" James both graduated from St. Vincent–St. Mary High School, decades apart, and Giffels sees the Black Keys' climb as analogous to that of James's rise to fame: "One very important parallel is both Dan, Pat, and LeBron were all born right at the beginning of the Rust Belt years of the real hard times [1980, 1979, and 1984, respectively]. LeBron, when he came back [to Cleveland], he wrote that essay in *Sports Illustrated* where he says, 'In Northeast Ohio, nothing is given. Everything is earned.'[4] That's straight from what they grew up in. You have to work hard and fight and pay tons of dues more because you're from here than if you're from somewhere else. And that's how LeBron and the Black Keys have crafted their careers."

When Carney and Auerbach ditched Akron for Nashville, their departure left some locals feeling salty. "People get opinionated about it because people in Akron say so many other bands in Akron were better than the Black Keys at that time," Jeri Sapronetti says. "Their early stuff was good. I used to hate on them a little bit but only because I was jealous. 'You guys are living the ultimate fantasy.' If I were me and had some money, I would build some awesome venue we need. Nashville's not that great."

The rock revivalists' ascension stunned other Akronites, like Devo's Jerry Casale. "I thought it was mindboggling how big they got when what they were doing was Jack White and the White Stripes part two," he says. "Like, okay, we're going to start playing songs without bass just like the White Stripes. It's just incredible. They persisted. They toured their butts off, and when they finally had hits, they added a bass."

Susan Schmidt Horning, from former Akron trio Chi-Pig, also was gobsmacked at their achievements. "Ultimately, how many of these bands reach a point where they get the attention that the Black Keys got?" she says. "Everybody was shocked—wow, they're so popular. Even Pat's dad—he is a friend—said he couldn't believe it. He kept shaking his head because they'd done so well. It's interesting how they're a duo but they can make such huge music."

Yet Chuck isn't so bewildered. According to him, he always had a lot of faith in them, especially in their indefatigable work ethic. "I grew up with a guy in New Jersey who was a successful rock and roll musician in the nineteen seventies and is still playing music today," Auerbach says. "He's still one of the best rock guitarists I've ever seen, and I knew from watching him that anything was possible. So there was no reason if Dan worked hard enough he couldn't also be successful. And by the way, my definition of success is you get to do what you love."

Dan and Pat also love producing other artists' music. Dan won a Producer of the Year Grammy in 2013 for *El Camino* and Dr. John's *Locked Down*. He produced a record from Cincinnati's Buffalo Killers and the Pretenders' 2016 record, *Alone*. Pat has produced Michelle Branch and the band Tennis, and composed the theme song to the adult animated sitcom *BoJack Horseman* with his uncle Ralph Carney, saxophonist for the band Tin Huey. Ralph passed away in December 2017. The Black Keys decamped in 2015 to pursue other endeavors, such as Dan's solo projects and side bands.

"Dan is the busiest person I've seen in my life," says Brian Olive, a *Locked Down* collaborator and Cincinnati musician. "He's a workaholic. He never stops. It took him four days to text me back." Giffels says, "They made it by working their asses off and getting records out quick and not fussing around in the studio and just bashing it out and paying tons and tons of dues that I just don't think bands do anymore."

Dan's parents moved to Nashville to be closer to him, but after five years there Chuck and Mary moved back to Akron so that Chuck could start his music career. "There's fifty or a hundred great guitar players in Nashville, and you can't go anywhere in that town without tripping on one," Auerbach says. "But that doesn't mean you can get your stuff done with them. In Akron I find musicians to be more amenable to working with me the way that I want to work. In a place like Nashville, you are a small fish in a big pond. In Akron the pond is a lot smaller, but you have a better chance of getting things done."

A small sign posted in Akron's Lock 3 Park reads "Home of Grammy Award Winners the Black Keys." "Signs like that are nice for tourists and for young kids to see, but if you're an artist, you're always trying to do the next thing," Chuck Auerbach says. "If you judge an artist's success by Grammys and their bank account, I think you're missing the point. What they're going to do in the future—that's what is always on their minds. It is a struggle, but art is a struggle in a society that doesn't value art." He knows the guys have influenced a lot of local musicians to work hard and trust themselves. "They've been a kind of inspiration in the same way LeBron has been inspirational for a lot of young men and women in this town."

No other Ohio-born and -raised band had made the mark that the Black Keys did in the early twenty-first century. Columbus's Twenty One Pilots, yet another duo, won a Grammy in 2017, but they rocketed in the age of social media, unlike the Black Keys' humble beginnings. "I think the Black Keys will be regarded as the last American band to just start a band, to get a van and start from the bottom and start driving to cities and playing shows and putting out records more or less on their own, and going from that point to stadium headliner," Giffels says. "I don't think that can happen again. So they're an anomaly in that way."

## CHI-PIG

*There was a sense of challenge—can girls really do this?*

—Susan Schmidt Horning

Naming a band after a BBQ joint with a cute pig-with-wings logo seems very Ohio, which is what the boy-girl Akron trio Chi-Pig did in the 1970s. Susan Schmidt Horning, Debbie Smith, and Richard Roberts formed Chi-Pig in 1977. They were a faction in the sea of

Akron bands that received attention from bigger cities, but unlike their cohorts Tin Huey and Devo, they had no major labels come calling. "If you had a band and you wanted to do that for a living, at that time you had to get signed to a label," Horning says. "Chi-Pig had that goal more in our twenties. It was disappointing we didn't get a record deal." However, she was happy for her friends who did get signed. Chi-Pig's song "Apu Api (Help Me)" appeared on the 1978 album *The Akron Compilation* and (along with "Ring Around the Collar") on 2015's *Punk 45: Burn Rubber City, Burn! Akron, Ohio: Punk and the Decline of the Mid-West 1975–80*. In 1979 the band recorded their debut record, the appropriately titled *Miami*, recorded in Miami, but it didn't get formally released until 2004. The band played shows in Akron, Cleveland, and Kent, and some in New York City, where they met avant-garde impresario Klaus Nomi. "His manager asked if there was much of a [music] scene in Ohio, and I said, 'Sure, there's this club we play at all the time, the Bank. You think Klaus would go?' So we brought Klaus Nomi to Akron, and that was his first gig west of the Hudson River. That was fun."

Chi-Pig fit nicely into the weird New Wave bands emerging from Akron in the late seventies and early eighties. A communal force existed among the Akron rock groups, with many of them sharing bills at the Bank and at JB's in Kent. "Everything in retrospect seems to have a brighter glow to it somehow," Horning says. "The fact that there was this club that we could all play in was important, because if that hadn't existed, I don't know if we would've had so much contact with each other." She describes their live shows as "lively," but they struggled to generate a big sound. "I wished we would've taken on more musicians, because we could've done more musically. We were tight as a trio, though."

Chi-Pig featured two female musicians, which seemed atypical for that time. (The Waitresses also had more than one female.) Horning is doing research for a book on all-girl rock bands and wonders, "Why didn't these women get recognized? There were a whole lot of bands I've learned about that nobody ever heard of except in their local area, because I think record companies have been sexist and male dominated forever and just didn't know what to do with girls playing instruments."

Horning says Chi-Pig and her previous band the Poor Girls were accepted because "we played well." "I'm not saying we were brilliant—I know I wasn't—but we were serious about playing well. There was a sense of challenge—can girls really do this? And then they'd hear us play. There's always that sense of having to demonstrate we could do it, but we were doing that anyway because we simply wanted to be good at what we did. But we were always considered special, that idea of oh, it's an all-girl band, so you're treated in special way, not because you necessarily wanted to be treated that way, but because you're unusual. You're a novelty."

Horning had been treated as even more special when in 1965 she, Smith, Pam Johnson, and Esta Kerr assembled the Poor Girls, while they were still in junior high school. As far as Horning knows, the Poor Girls were Akron's first all-girl rock band. The seed was planted when the women took guitar lessons from a guy named Joe Ciriello. "He said, 'Why don't you girls start a band?' So we're like, why not?" In the beginning they played instrumental versions of surf-rock songs. As teenagers they played gigs in clubs, even though they were underage. "Our parents had to give permission to our manager," she says. "He was really great. He not only got us the gigs; he drove us, he picked us up, he put the equipment in the van. Those were the days when you rented a U-Haul trailer and attached it to the back of your car to put your equipment in it."

Devo liked one of Chi-Pig's song's, "Temple on My Plan," which became Devo's "Gates of Steel." "We had copyrighted it, and when Mark [Mothersbaugh] told Debbie, 'Hey, you remember that thing you were jamming on in Sue's basement? Why don't we turn it into a song?' And she said, 'It's already a song.' They changed the lyrics but the chord progression was our song." Even though Sue and Debbie didn't sit down with Devo and pen the song, Devo shared songwriting credit and they still receive royalties from it.

Music today isn't what it was back then. Because young people didn't want to work in factories, Horning thinks, it led to "people picking up electric guitars and drum sets and forming bands in the sixties." "You have to consider that time, broadly speaking, when there weren't all these other things that took people's attention like the internet and video games," she says. "Obviously there's still a lot of groups playing, making their own records, and coming up from nowhere with just grassroots support. It's different. Then, that was the only game in town, and now there's so many other things to distract people."

After Horning graduated from high school, she briefly attended Brooklyn College of Music but dropped out and moved back to Akron. Once Chi-Pig finally disbanded in the fall of 1980, she returned to New York. Ralph Carney had her play on a song for his band the Swollen Monkeys. "Ralph said, 'Sue, can you play bass?' I borrowed Chris Butler's bass and I practiced real hard and filled in for a bit." She worked at a record label and then stopped playing music altogether. "I didn't play in another band again," she says. "I got married and everything went to shit after that. I got very delusional with the music business when I started working for a record company." Done with music, Horning took the academic path. She got her bachelor's degree in her thirties, at the University of Akron, and ended up with a PhD in her fifties, from Case Western Reserve. Since 2007 she has taught history courses at St. John's University in New York, and in 2013 she published a book on audio recording called *Chasing Sound.*[5] "I love what I do, but I don't think I have the passion for it that I did for music," she says. "Then again, I'm a lot older than I was when I was a musician full-time."

Music briefly wrestled its way into her life again in 2004 when she and Chi-Pig played a few gigs in support of *Miami* finally being self-released. "I wish I could go back," she says. "It was fun, it was work, but you're consumed with it. Doing music is one of the greatest things, and I regret I didn't somehow make it more a part of my life. It's hard as an academic to do it, even when you're studying musical topics. In my case, they sort of interfere with each other. It's also a matter of you're young, you're single, you don't have responsibilities. What's not to like?"

## DEVO

*You probably couldn't find a band that's more misunderstood than Devo.*

—Jerry Casale

No other band from Ohio will leave behind the rock heritage that Devo will. The Akron group hasn't been nominated for entry into the Rock and Roll Hall of Fame. They've only been nominated for one Grammy, in 1985, for a music video collection. Yet as cofounder Jerry Casale explains to me, "We were the most conceptual band to ever come out of Ohio," and that's one reason why the band is both lauded and misunderstood.

The band formed in the early seventies at Kent State University, soon after the horrific Kent State shootings on May 4, 1970, which left four students dead, including friends of the band. Jerry Casale and Bob Lewis invented the idea of "de-evolution," or society's penchant to de-evolve into stupidity. "We came up with this whole thing, and it was a philosophy and an art movement," Casale says. He persuaded artist Mark Mothersbaugh to join the group, too. "We brainwashed Mark with Devo epistemology and it spoke to him," he says. "We were all outsiders who felt the same way about what we were witnessing. That's when I got the idea to make Devo music." Mark's brother Bob joined the group, and so did Alan Myers and Jerry's brother, also named Bob. (Myers died in 2013 and Bob Casale died in 2014.)

"They basically built an alternative universe," Chris Butler says. "It had its own language. It had its own symbols and symbiotics and certainly had its own original music. I think that's all a reaction in trying to crack that Northeast Ohio holy triumvirate."

Once the band gelled, they decided their music had to be completely original, though inspired by Captain Beefheart and electronic musician Morton Subotnick. "If it sounded like what was already going on, if it sounded formulaic, we jettisoned it," Casale says. "We only moved forward with something new." That entailed using odd instruments like a harp and a mini-Moog, and writing lyrics that weren't just about seducing women. "We did it consciously," he says. "It was very on purpose."

It's true their music is unclassifiable. It's not punk. It's not New Wave. It's just "Devo music." "It's like Parliament-Funkadelic—what else is Parliament Funk? What else is Jimi Hendrix except Jimi Hendrix?" Casale says.

> We didn't mind being called punk, because we were in the movement enough to be responding to current events, and we had the intensity and anger shared with punk. But punk could be anti-intellectual and nihilistic, and Devo wasn't like that. We were offering up ideas. We were offering up alternatives to the morass that people found themselves in. We were trying to explain to people they had to take responsibility by thinking for themselves and questioning illegitimate authority. Certainly coming out of Kent State after the hideous Vietnam War and the killings of May 4 and the kind of governor we had, it was a civil war.

Decades later, Casale's political ideology remains fierier than ever. We talk about the advent of the Trump administration and how the concept of de-evolution was finally occurring. "It was a warning," Casale says. "We didn't think all of this would really happen. Now it went beyond our worst fears. I don't know if you know about Mike Judge's movie *Idiocracy*, but *Idiocracy* is the movie Devo should've made—and I think we would've made it better. That was a movie about what happens when de-evolution occurs. And now with the world the way it is, and this ridiculous unqualified Trumpolini guy, who is anathema to democracy, what we have is beyond *Idiocracy*." He's a bit disappointed no one asked Devo to play the inauguration, because they would've participated. That is, as a means to protest. "We would've gladly taken the heat by saying what we're doing here is celebrating the triumph of de-evolution. All we would've had to do was play 'Jocko Homo,' 'Beautiful World,' and 'Freedom of Choice.' Those songs are timeless."

When Casale isn't Devo-ing, he's a vintner. He owns the 50 by 50 winery in Napa Valley and bottles pinot noirs. I ask him why so many bands have emerged from Ohio, and he goes into a wine metaphor. "It's like growing wine: the vines that produce the greatest fruit are the ones that are the most 'stressed'—that is, they are in soil on terrace land that's highly mineral and volcanic—so the roots have to dig real deep to find the water, and it produces better-tasting fruit. So that's why there's so many: because it's that do-or-die thing. It's a field of battle. You're forced to really get strong or you go down."

In the late 1970s the band found their moxie, signed with Warner Bros., and moved to Los Angeles, where Casale still lives. Though Casale hasn't lived in Akron in decades, he speaks fondly of his buds back in Northeast Ohio. "I like the particularly unique personality of Ohio creative people, because they're not pretentious," he says. "They all grew up with hard knocks surrounded by a prevailing culture that was anti-creative and anti-liberal. If you were different at all—which most creative people with fresh ideas are—you were marginalized and threatened, and even beat up. Some of the greatest art is born of trauma. This gives you the fortitude to plow ahead, because you're not in this groovy metropolis like New York or San Francisco. You work in isolation against all odds when you're from Ohio, and you have to learn to believe in yourself, and you have to persevere."

In 1977 UK-based Stiff Records released Devo's three-song record *B Stiff*, which included a cover of the Rolling Stones' "Satisfaction," done Devo-style. (Devo was one of the first American bands to use a lot of synthesizers in their music.) A year later, in 1978, they released the full-length *Q: Are We Not Men? A: We Are Devo!*, featuring the band wearing their signature red Energy Domes. It went gold and peaked at seventy-three on the charts. Next came 1979's *Duty Now for the Future*, and in 1980 they found wild acclaim with *Freedom of Choice*, which performed better—number twenty-two on the charts and platinum sales. The album birthed their highest-charting US single, "Whip It," a career-defining song that's been used in everything from a Swiffer commercial to the movie *Romy and Michele's High School Reunion*. Though the S&M-themed song is their most recognizable, it's not their best. For instance, "Gut Feeling," "That's Good," "Gates of Steel," and many others are better representations of their eclectic sound.

Despite their achievements, people didn't quite get Devo. "You probably couldn't find a band that's more misunderstood than Devo," Casale says. "I remember as we were becoming more and more successful and famous, the critics were so mean to us and hated us. They either thought we were clowns, or they thought we were fascists, or fascist clowns, which was funny. They didn't like our music. They said we couldn't play. They said we couldn't sing. It's ridiculous. We could really play and we could really sing."

In 2003 David Giffels published the definitive book on Devo, *We Are DEVO!*, in which he and coauthor Jade Dellinger interviewed the band about their rise to the top, starting with chronicling their days before Kent State.[6] "That subject had been around, for me, for a long time," Giffels says on why he wanted to write about the ensemble. "Devo was so closely associated with Akron, not because they're from here, but because they used so much of the aesthetic and the culture that I associated with in their music."

Giffels states that even though Devo became mainstream, they still telegraphed Ohio's DIY mind-set. "Even at its most evolved, Devo still seemed like something that they threw together in a garage. But there was something about it that seemed handmade and directly from the creative energy of the people who were in it."

Devo released a few more records but between 1990 and 2010 took a long break from releasing new material. In 2008 they played their first Akron show in thirty years, in support of electing Barack Obama (they shared the stage with Chrissie Hynde and the Black Keys). In 2009 they toured with albums *Are We Not Men?* and *Freedom of Choice*, playing both in their entireties. In 2010, twenty years after the release of *Smooth Noodle Maps*, they finally released new material with *Something for Everybody*, which topped at number thirty on the charts. Because the band headlined a lot of music festivals, a younger generation discovered them for the first time.

"There would be two or three generations crowding around the stage to see Devo," Casale says. "Millennials learned about us from YouTube." But the shows didn't ignite the same fervor that Devo's shows did back in the day, when their shows were "legendary." When they played at the Universal Amphitheatre in Los Angeles, Casale says, "the energy was just so over the top." The production value of the shows entailed a video wall, costumes, and Mark Mothersbaugh putting on a baby mask as his alter ego Booji Boy. Casale talks about a festival they played once outside of London, to a crowd of four hundred thousand haters. "They tried to throw things at us, but the stage, because it was a festival, the stage was so high and the people were far enough back that when they'd throw things, the things would fall short and hit other people in the crowd. So we were watching people fight with each other. It was massive booing, but we kind of got off on it. We'd liked being lightning rods for hostility, because we were new and they were there to see these old classic acts, like Lynyrd Skynyrd."

Despite the polemic responses, Casale says he misses those bygone days. "I loved engaging with the culture on that level. Whether you were liked, loved, or hated, it didn't make any difference. Something big was happening and it felt really exciting."

As of this writing, Devo is on hiatus. Casale sounds frustrated, almost defeated, when he discusses how Mark Mothersbaugh would rather focus on his film music career—he has composed scores for Wes Anderson films—than regrouping the art collective. "Mark Mothersbaugh turned his back on that," he says. "He churns out soundtrack music because he can make a lot of money. He's not applying himself to the aesthetics that make Devo; otherwise we'd be out there right now securing our legacy. What better time for Devo to show up in the midst of this firestorm of America unraveling, with songs that are more relevant now than they have been since Reagan?"

Casale is skeptical of the band's legacy and thinks he could've accomplished more. "Devo wasn't skinny ties and white shirts," he says. "Each album sounded different. I had a movie ready to go but I never got to make it. There's a documentary sitting on a shelf. I wanted to do a musical, and I really hit all of the mediums and [tried to] make it more obvious to people what Devo was about, which is a big picture thing. I wanted Devo to be beyond the cult of personality. I really did."

A few days after I talk to Casale, something strange happens. He made it sound like Devo was going to leave behind an effete memory. At the rock-themed beer bar Hop Cat in Louisville, the owner had saved all of his concert tickets, dating back to the seventies. He preserved them under the bar's glass top. I sat at the bar, and what concert ticket did I sit in front of? Devo, circa 1979. The ticket was surrounded by stubs from the Grateful Dead, the Stones, and AC/DC. Seeing this display put things in perspective for me—Devo was just as good, if not better, than those bands. They found a place at the rock and roll table. Then a couple of weeks later I watched the Oscar-nominated film *20th Century Women*, starring Annette Bening and Greta Gerwig. The movie takes place in 1979, so it has a heavy punk and post-punk soundtrack. Gerwig's character wears a Devo sweatshirt, and their song "Gut Feeling" plays on the soundtrack alongside tracks by Talking Heads, Iggy Pop, and Bowie. Again I realized they had sealed their place in the annals of rock history. Devo may be misunderstood, but I have a (gut) feeling that decades from now, critics and fans alike will appreciate their requisite contributions to the art and political spheres.

Casale isn't the only one who's confused as to why Devo has been passed over for a Hall of Fame nomination. During the 2017 Hall of Fame induction of Pearl Jam, bassist Jeff Ament wore a self-made T-shirt listing all the musical groups the organization has overlooked, including Nine Inch Nails, Guided by Voices, and our dear Devo. However, non–Hall of Fame judges give Devo respect every summer in Cleveland when the Beachland Ballroom hosts DEVOtional, a weekend-long tribute to the band, which Casale has attended.

"We were never trying to be trendy, and there was always substance behind the songs," Casale says on why the band has lasted for so long. "A lot of the songs endure because there's something timeless about them, even if the sound is somewhat locked in time. Bob Dylan's 'Like a Rolling Stone'—it definitely sounds like when it was from. But it's just as powerful now as it was then. I would like our legacy to be that we were what was *new* about New Wave. We fought a good fight for a long time."

### THE PRETENDERS

*We hung out on her tour bus and she gave me a pizza and*
*showed me her bunk. She's real goofy and silly.*

—Jeri Sapronetti

Do we classify the Pretenders as an Akron band if only one of the four founding members grew up there? Front woman Chrissie Hynde had to move to London—twice—for the band to finally coalesce. But Hynde is a bona fide Ohioan. One of her first band experiences was playing with Devo's Mark Mothersbaugh (also from Akron) in the band Sat. Sun. Mat. In her 2015 memoir, *Reckless: My Life as a Pretender,* she writes about being so shy she locked herself in Mothersbaugh's laundry room and performed sitting on the dryer.[7] The uninhibited memoir spills her life from growing up in a normal (but strict) Akron family to hitting the jackpot with the Pretenders in England. She discusses Akron in detail, from the fertile heyday of when the city lived up to its Rubber Capital of the World title to the decline in industry by the time she left for Kent State. She has a funny passage about driving Bowie in her mother's car the first time he played Cleveland. She vents about her frustration in trying to form a band and writes that the prospects seemed "laughable"— until the late 1970s in England.

Hynde's childhood friend Susan Schmidt Horning remembers "Chris." "We were born three days apart," she says. "We've known each other since grade school, and we hung out in high school." Hynde wasn't playing in a band when she observed Chi-Pig and other groups in town. "Chris came to one of our gigs," Horning says. "There were a lot of girls, I think, who had the same admiration for rock bands that boys had: Why shouldn't we play? Why should it be any different?"

"I like Chrissie Hynde," Filter front man Richard Patrick says. "Her usage of vibrato is so intense that it's almost like a distraction, but it's so perfectly done. And her attitude—she has a fuck you attitude, and I love that. I think that attitude is part of that Ohio scene—'We're never going to make it, so fuck you.'"

During her second move to London, Hynde got more involved in the punk scene there and formed the Pretenders when she found kindred spirits in three men: drummer Martin Chambers, guitarist James Honeyman-Scott, and bassist Pete Farndon. They recorded a cover of the Kinks' "Stop Your Sobbing," released in 1979. They signed to Sire Records, which released their eponymous record stateside in 1980. It shot to number one on the UK charts and performed almost as well in the United States. A year later they released their sophomore album, *Pretenders II*; 1984's *Learning to Crawl* gave them their best showing on the US charts. "The Pretenders were more hard rock," Chris Butler says. "They weren't a weirdo band, even though she did things in 7/8 time. It sounded like traditional hard rock."

However, it didn't take long for misfortune to transpire. Honeyman-Scott died of heart failure induced by cocaine in 1982, and eight months later Farndon injected a speedball into his arm and drowned in the bathtub. The band reconvened and marched forward with different lineups throughout the years.

During Thanksgiving weekend of 2016, I traveled to Akron—my mom's hometown—to see the sold-out Pretenders concert at the University of Akron's E. J. Thomas Hall. I hadn't seen them live before and thought it would be important to see Hynde perform in front of twenty-nine hundred of her hometown fans. One thing I can say about the Pretenders is they're punctual. They started on time and played for exactly ninety minutes. Their 2016 LP, *Alone*, was produced by fellow Akronite Dan Auerbach, and *Alone* is the song they opened with. Hynde was graced with a pink tuxedo jacket and wore an Elvis T-shirt underneath. Chambers was there, and so were younger bandmates James Walbourne, bassist Nick Wilkinson, and a pedal-steel player. Hynde sang most of her hits—"Message of Love," "Back on the Chain Gang," "Stop Your Sobbing," "Middle of the Road," "I'll Stand by You," "Don't Get Me Wrong"—and the blues-funk song about her birthplace, "My City Was Gone." "I'm not going to be nice because I'm back home," she joked. The twenty-song set list emphasized just how many memorable songs the band has in their canon. I know it's ageism to say, "Well into her sixties, Hynde's still got her puckish punk spirit," but it's the truth. It's understandable why the Pretenders were inducted into the Hall of Fame.

As much as Hynde and company impressed me, the band's opener, Time Cat, took me by surprise. Lead singer Jeri Sapronetti's wailing voice was reminiscent of Erika Wennerstrom of the Heartless Bastards. One listen to Time Cat's song "Boozled" and you'll know what I mean. It turns out Jeri's a Chrissie Hynde superfan.

Sapronetti explained to me how she got to open for one of her idols. In July 2016 a BBC film crew followed Hynde to Akron for Punk Week. World-famous photographer Jill Furmanovsky premiered a punk-rock photo exhibit at 22 High Street Gallery at the Uncorked Wine Bar, and Sapronetti's friend needed to book a band for the evening. "My friend didn't know what to do for the opening night," Sapronetti says. Knowing Chrissie, the BBC, and Furmanovsky would be gathered in one room, Sapronetti demanded that her friend "put us in there." Time Cat played the opening night reception, but Hynde didn't make an appearance until after their gig was over. "My friend, she was so upset because she was really pulling for us," Sapronetti says. "It's hard to get good opportunities like that. Finally when we can get some help in the rock and roll world, she doesn't show up." However, Sapronetti met Hynde after the show on the wine bar's patio, although people swarmed Hynde, which made it difficult to talk. "I'm sitting in a semicircle with the BBC, that photographer, and Chrissie," Sapronetti says. "It was so surreal. I completely suppressed all my need to freak out. I told myself, 'I'm just going to play it cool.'"

A couple of weeks later the BBC emailed Sapronetti saying Hynde wanted to talk to her. "Apparently Chrissie looked up all of our stuff and thought it was amazing," Sapronetti says. "She said crazy things like we 'brought her home' and 'restored her faith in rock and roll music.' She said all of these nice things that shocked me. We emailed back and forth for a while." Hynde hinted to Sapronetti that she and the Pretenders would possibly play a show in Akron. "I heard this commercial on the radio that announced the Pretenders at E. J. Thomas. I immediately emailed Chrissie and wrote, 'Oh, E. J. Thomas, huh? That's pretty cool.' And she wrote back, 'Oh, let me talk with my people and see if I can get you on the show.' The next day [her people] are like, 'Hey, do you want to play?'"

Sapronetti, Sam Caler, and Colten Huffman have released a few albums and have played gigs around Akron, Cleveland, and Cincinnati. Although they opened for actress-singer Juliette Lewis once, the E. J. Thomas show was their biggest crowd and most high-profile show of their neophyte career. "After reading her memoir, I thought, 'she's lived a life similar to mine,'" Sapronetti says. "We went to all the same schools growing up in Akron. We're just weirdos growing up."

When Jeri and Hynde were vis-à-vis in a quieter setting, Jeri said she felt "nervous." "We hung out on her tour bus and she gave me a pizza and showed me her bunk. She's real goofy and silly. I've heard a lot of negative talk about her my whole life. It seemed everyone was mad at her because she would say bad things about Akron. It upset people. She's argumentative and a punk rocker. I think she's misunderstood. She was really nice to us. She was concerned about the temperature of our dressing room and made sure we were happy. She called me 'Jer.' It was really strange."

The euphoric experience of opening for the Pretenders led Jeri to consider what was next. "There's so much leading up to a show," she says. "What do you do now? You want to top yourself and up your game somehow. For me, the Chrissie Hynde thing, that was luck."

Some locals may be bruised that she got out of Dodge and headed for stardom in England, but Hynde nourished her Akron roots. In 2007 she opened a vegan restaurant in the city, but it shuttered four years later. In 2008 she joined Devo and the Black Keys at a pro-Obama show at Akron Civic Theatre. Basically, rock and roll icon Chris Hynde never left her city behind.

### TIN HUEY // THE NUMBERS BAND // THE WAITRESSES

*In Ohio we have chips on our shoulders.*

—Chris Butler

Like Jerry Casale, Chris Butler attended Kent State and immersed himself in the music scene around campus. While growing up in Cleveland, Butler performed in a high school band and cradled that experience at university. The city's Water Street, he says, had a slew of bars that booked original live music, including his groups 15-60-75 the Numbers Band and Tin Huey. "It was unheard of to have all of these bars with original bands," Butler says. "You had this place where people could play and an audience who wanted to hear something new. Those were great elements to make up a helluva scene."

The May 4, 1970, shootings, he says, demonstrated that "one couldn't be part of a system that tried to kill you. So what are you going to do? You're going to build an alternative," and it happened to be based in music and art.

"Dave Thomas of [Cleveland band] Pere Ubu talked a lot about this," Butler says. "He said there were the artists and the rockers. If you wanted to be in a band, you had to play with people who were not into what you were into. You were a majority of one. And out of that came a lot of originality."

Butler joined the ongoing Numbers Band as bassist with Bob Kidney and Terry Hynde (Chrissie's brother). "That was a great training ground," Butler says. "That's another factor from the area—you cannot discount the huge impact of Bob and Jack Kidney and Terry Hynde. They played original music from the jump. It was blues-based, but what they did with it was from another planet. Bob's work ethic was life or death. They were the gold standard for being accepted as themselves. That rubbed off on all of us, and still does."

Jerry Casale, who also played bass in the band, agrees. "The Numbers Band became a Northeast Ohio institution and became something legendary and nonpareil," he explains. "There's nobody who followed their arc of music and does what they do now. They're still playing with some of the guys who were playing when I was in the band."

Casale's former Numbers bandmate Chris Butler recognizes the impact of Numbers and other Kent bands. "I've had many discussions with Jerry about what a remarkable scene we all grew up in Kent, and how the Numbers fueled it, and May 4 fueled it, and the opposition from the Cleveland triumvirate fired our ambitions to be bigger than just little local bands. In Ohio we have chips on our shoulders. We're also-rans in all of this popular culture stuff. And it makes us a little cranky. That puts an edge to the music and the sound. You want to be recognized."

The collective mainly stuck to playing live shows in Kent, Akron, and Cleveland and didn't sign to a major label. Butler, who then moved to Akron, focused on Tin Huey and signed a two-record deal with Warner Bros. In 1979 the band—including Ralph Carney and Harvey Gold—released the LP *Contents Dislodged during Shipment*. There may or may not have been some dissent in the Akron/Kent community when Tin Huey got signed and the Numbers did not. "I know I ran into a lot of trouble with Bob Kidney for years," Butler says. An A&R (artists and repertoire) rep came to see Tin Huey play at JB's in Kent, and the Numbers were also playing that night. Butler sang the Numbers' praises, but the rep didn't want to see them.

Many people in the community felt that Tin Huey snatched the Numbers' potential record contract. "There were some hard feelings there for a long time," Butler says. "Things changed when someone got a record deal, because you get the 'why not me?' thing."

After middling returns on Tin Huey's album, Warner Bros. bought the band out instead of releasing another record with them. Butler struck out on his own with a Kent bar singer named Patty Donahue. He describes her as a spirited and spunky "girl around town," who "was plucked from the bar scene and put on stage and frankly deserved to be there," he says. "But I could see how someone would go, 'Man, he formed a band around this woman who did not spend her dues toiling in the clubs.'" The two, along with Ralph Carney, recorded the New Wave-y song "I Know What Boys Like" in 1979—which was the impetus for Butler's move to the Big Apple.

"I had a song that people thought was going to be a hit," he says about why he left Rubber City. "I loved New York. I was tired of doing the DIY thing, because it was clear that in the Akron area you had to build with your own structure—and yet it was all right there in New York. The odds were it was going to be easier [in New York]." Butler wrote the song based on his own humiliating experiences in the dating pool. "I had a record contract with Tin Huey and I couldn't hook up," he says. "I went to New York and I was liked and appreciated."

He had no ambitions to join a band—he was a songwriter—but when he presented the track to DJ Mark Kamins, who gave the acetate copy to Island Records, the label asked, "Where is your band, Butler?" He had no other choice than to employ players.

"The band was not my first choice of professions," he says. "It was very hard work. We were older. We weren't nineteen-year-olds and wanting to get laid and take drugs and ride in a limousine. We wanted careers. We were bumping in thirty. And these were experienced players."

Butler met Don Christensen, who had a recording studio. Island wanted the band to record a B-side to "Boys" so they could distribute it on their ZE subsidiary (for founders Michael Zilkha and Michel Esteban). "I mailed my last fifty bucks to Patty for a bus ticket, and she left her boyfriend at the Greyhound station in Cleveland and came to New York. We booked a studio and we recorded the song 'No Guilt.'"

Most of the musicians in the newly conceived Waitresses were from the Midwest, including bassist Dave Hofstra (Kansas) and saxophonist Mars Williams (Chicago). Now an eight-piece—which included three women—the band set sail to conquer New York. In 1982 the group released their debut full-length record, *Wasn't Tomorrow Wonderful?* It included "Boys" and "No Guilt" and climaxed at number forty-one on the Billboard chart. That same year they released the five-song EP *I Could Rule the World if I Could Only Get the Parts*, featuring the *Square Pegs* TV theme song they composed, along with the track they'd most be associated with, the infectious earworm "Christmas Wrapping," which plays ad nauseam on radio and in stores every December.

"I am the proverbial Scrooge and Grinch combined," Butler says, "but I have to say that I have softened over the years and I'm goddamn grateful. I finally had my moment. I'm in the supermarket [in Akron] and it played over the PA system. It sounds pretty good on tinny speakers. I sat there and said, 'I wrote that song!' to a couple people with shopping carts, and they gave me a funny look."

In 1983 the band released *Bruiseology*, their final record together, and in 1984 the group dissolved. "You put five years into something, every day," Butler says about the end of the Waitresses. "It was terrible." Although the Waitresses' output was short-lived, Butler thinks they made an impact.

> Patty was not a rock chic. She wasn't a folky. She was a different kind of woman—an "every girl." There was nobody really talking to the secretaries and the middle management women. They weren't represented in popular song. I was very aware of feminism and how that was changing everything. This was the eighties. This is "you can have it all." This is "I don't need a man." All of that was very much in the zeitgeist of the time: female empowerment

and my own desire to learn about women, because, like any other dumb guy, I wanted to know the score. As a writer, I wanted to know what's going on in a woman's mind.

Patty Donahue died in 1996, at age forty, from lung cancer. Butler, Gold, and Carney formed the group Half Cleveland, and Butler still reaps royalties from the Waitresses. In 2015 he moved from New York back to Akron—he owns Jeffrey Dahmer's childhood house, which, surprisingly, does not look a murder house—because "everything I went there for is gone. It's too expensive. You can't have clubs." Butler says with the way the record industry is structured today, he can't imagine giving it a go now. "It was always awful, but now it's brutal." Yet he's not bitter. Okay, well, maybe cantankerous. "I'm very happy with the little bit of success I've had," he says. "I'm able to have a modest income. I'm able to keep working. I never reached the limousine, heavy-duty-drug-habit level. I never needed a bodyguard. Once a year, the Christmas thing—it makes a helluva a lot of people happy. Maybe that's as good as it gets."

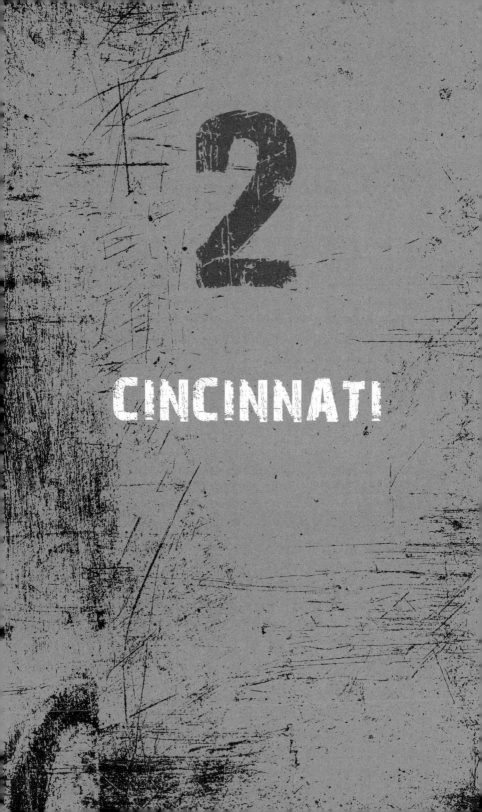

# 2

# CINCINNATI

UNTIL 1790 CINCINNATI WAS NAMED LOSANTIVILLE. ALMOST
two hundred years later, in the late 1970s, Jerry Springer was mayor.
But those are trivial facts and have nothing to do with music. Cincy
may be located on the cusp of the South, but its sound is pure Midwest. The Queen City, as it's known, has a rich history of R&B, blues,
and country acts dating back to the 1940s. King Records and Herzog
Records were two prominent recording studios/labels in town. The
former is known for James Brown stepping in and recording music,
the latter for Hank Williams putting "Lovesick Blues" on tape. It
wasn't until the 1980s that rock bands like the Wolverton Brothers
and Afghan Whigs began to alter the modern sound. In the twenty-
first century, there isn't a specific "Cincinnati Sound" like there was
in the 1940s–1970s, as chronicled in Randy McNutt's book of the
same name.[1] "There's always been a rich tradition of music from
here," says Chuck Cleaver of local bands Wussy and the Ass Ponys. "I
think it was overlooked for a while. I think it was strong in the fifties
and sixties, and then nobody paid any attention."

"There wasn't some hit factory that was grooming bands or turning stuff out that established a certain sound like a Motown or

something like that," says Mike Montgomery, a stalwart on the indie scene. "From the early nineties to now, I think there's so many studios, so many clubs, so many bands. It has really diversified. There is not one company or one studio controlling what goes in and what goes out."

Darren Blase, a gormandizer of music and co-owner of Cincinnati's Shake It Records, remembers a time before the Afghan Whigs when power-pop reigned supreme. "Before that, the bands that had the most success were the Raisins [Covington, Kentucky, native and King Crimson guitarist Adrian Belew produced their 1983 eponymous debut album], or the Modulators," he says. "They weren't ready-for-prime-time kind of bands. I think now it's a different industry. I think now it's more artist driven than label driven."

"I think Cincinnati is understated," local musician Brian Olive says. "People are understated. They don't brag about it. They don't boast about it. It's not crammed in everybody's faces. Not every band from Ohio is the biggest band in the world, but some of them could be. Some of them are."

Olive talks about old venues he used to play, including Sudsy Malone's Rock 'n Roll Laundry and Bar, which was part music venue and part Laundromat. "Sudsy Malone's was the best place ever and it's probably because that where I started out. It was a great club." Sudsy's shuttered in 2008, but Bogart's, located across the street, lives on. The three-venues-in-one Southgate House—the former home of the guy who invented the Tommy Gun—had legal disputes in 2011. It temporarily closed but reopened down the street in October 2012 as the Southgate House Revival, located inside a church. "The old Southgate House was really cool to play," Olive says. "I wish they hadn't destroyed it. It's not the same to me." Former Southgate and Sudsy booker Dan McCabe opened the 150-person capacity MOTR Pub in the city's Over-the-Rhine district in 2010. Almost every night of the week they offer free shows. In 2014, across the street from MOTR, McCabe and team restored a one-hundred-year-old former theater—with a six-hundred-person capacity—and named it Woodward Theater.

Montgomery began his musical career in the late eighties and early nineties, when he noticed the audible whir around town. "This was when Sudsy's was happening," he says. "There were touring bands coming through every night of the week. It was real exciting. It was a real movement. There was a lot of energy to be in a band then. It was a real commitment or a life choice that you were going to make it work and book shows and cobble together the resources to make it happen."

The soulful R&B rock–inflected Afghan Whigs formed in the mid-eighties and self-released their first record, *Big Top Halloween*, in 1988. Two years later they signed to Seattle major indie label Sub Pop—one of the first bands outside of the Pacific Northwest to do so. Lead singer and songwriter Greg Dulli, John Curley, Rick McCollum, and Steve Earle set the mainstream Cincy rock scene in motion, which led to the bands Throneberry and the Ass Ponys getting signed to the majors, too. The Whigs signed to Elektra and released *Gentleman* in 1993. They disbanded in 2001 but reformed in 2012 and released more records on Sub Pop. "Right as the Afghan Whigs was about to sign a deal—that used to be a big word—there was a sense of pride on these older musicians that I would meet, that Cincinnati was a real thriving scene," Montgomery says. Montgomery grew up in Northern Kentucky and owns a recording studio in Cincinnati. He's been a part of the local fabric for a long time—he plays in bands Ampline and R. Ring, with Daytonian Kelley Deal.

If the Afghan Whigs was one of the most successful bands to hail from Cincinnati in the pre-internet era, then Walk the Moon could be viewed as the most successful Cincinnati group in the online era. "The Afghan Whigs—who else sounds like them? I don't know," Montgomery says. "There isn't another Cincinnati band that's aping the Whigs. That's their thing. The Whigs came up in Cincinnati and played with other local bands. They were very much a local band.

Walk the Moon—maybe I just wasn't clued in to them, but I don't re-member them living and breathing and having roots here. I feel like they were from here and had a meteoric rise and left. In my opinion, I wouldn't say they're a Cincinnati export." He considers authentic Cincinnati bands to be those who "live and die here," and "maybe bands that didn't jump here to next best thing. Alone at 3AM— that's a band that's Cincinnati born and bred. They all live here. That's a Midwest workingman's band. [The scene] is a network of people who are in it because they don't know how else to live a life."

To be fair, the members of Walk the Moon are Cincy natives. Their shows are frenetic, with fans wearing enough face paint to be mistaken for warriors. In the spring of 2015 they had a Billboard-charting hit with the song "Shut Up and Dance," which was a world-wide smash—it went number one in Poland, Canada, Colombia, and the United States. In 2012 guitarist Eli Maiman told me, "We love representing Cincinnati. We're extremely proud to have been from Cincinnati and we're going to keep repping it the best that we can." Their music is catchy as hell, and I hear it everywhere. I was in a bar in South Boston (of all places) and "Anna Sun" popped up on the jukebox. I was in the Dayton airport and "Shut Up" played on the PA system. Their music is inescapable.

"If you want to do music now in this town, there's no excuse," Montgomery says.

> There's something happening everywhere all the time. It didn't used to be like that. There were only maybe, at best, three clubs that would do original music. So to get in one of them was pretty hard for a while. You can go out seven days a week and hear a black metal sludge fest, and then you can have a weirdo shoegaze band at the next club, and you can have some art nerds playing a weird gallery show somewhere. In this town people do what they're going to do no matter what. As far as local bands from here, some have really lofty goals and some have no goal beyond hanging out, getting high, and playing guitar. It's everything in between.

Music festivals have sprung up in town, too. The inaugural Bun-bury Music Festival took place in July 2012 and has featured Ohio acts such as the Black Keys, Walk the Moon, Guided by Voices,

Foxy Shazam, Wussy, and the National. Every September the Mid-Point Music Festival takes over Over-the-Rhine; in 2014 the Afghan Whigs headlined one night of the fest, and in 2017 Walk the Moon headlined a night.

Grammy-winning the National is another band that has roots in Cincy. Matt Berninger, Aaron and Bryce Dessner, and Bryan and Scott Devendorf grew up there. Some of their family members still live in town; the Dessners curate the classical music fest MusicNOW every year and in April 2018, as part of MusicNOW, the National founded the annual two-day Homecoming music festival featuring several rock acts. However, the band officially formed in Brooklyn in 1999 and is considered more of a New York band than an Ohio band. (They do have a hit song called "Bloodbuzz Ohio.") The first time I saw the National play live was November 2005 at the one-hundred-person-capacity venue Schubas, in Chicago. They were touring in support of their breakthrough record, *Alligator*. By 2010 I saw them headline a festival in Portland, Oregon, and play coveted slots at Lollapalooza and the Pitchfork Festival. In 2013 they headlined the final night of Bunbury. In 2016, right before the presidential election, they played a free show in Cincinnati in support of Hillary Clinton. So maybe they aren't a homegrown Cincinnati band, but they're still a part of their old stomping ground.

## THE ASS PONYS // WUSSY

*We are one of those slow-burn bands that if we live long enough, we actually may make some money at it.*
—Chuck Cleaver

Wussy is a homegrown band, in the sense that all of the players are Cincinnati area or nearby Indiana natives. Front man Chuck Cleaver has been immersed in the scene since the late seventies and has lived in town since then. Local record store and label Shake It has distributed or co-distributed all of their records. They usually record their albums at local audio studio Ultrasuede, owned by the Whigs' John

Curley. But despite several critically acclaimed records—Robert Christgau of the *Village Voice* adores them, and in 2015 *Spin* magazine named their debut record, *Funeral Dress*, one of the top three hundred best records of the past thirty years—and a brief appearance on CBS *This Morning* in 2014 (their network TV debut), they aren't millionaires. Not even close. "We had no game plan," Cleaver says. "We didn't think, 'Let's make a bunch of money at this and let's be popular.'"

To appreciate the group, we must step back to the 1990s, when Cleaver was in the slightly more attention-getting group the Ass Ponies—Cleaver, Randy Cheek, Dave Morrison, and John Erhardt. The band signed to a major label (A&M) and had a minor radio hit with the twangy rock song "Little Bastard," from the 1994 album *Electric Rock Music*. "That was a fairly interesting time," Cleaver says. "I didn't understand it all that well. Different bands were getting signed and somehow Ass Ponies got in there, too. We kept telling them, 'We're not the next Nirvana. You're getting a bunch of uncooperative bastards. But if you want to sign us . . .'" Cleaver's partner in crime, Wussy bandmate Lisa Walker, asks Cleaver if he enjoyed being on a major. Cleaver says he did. "We got to go on tour, which we [had] never done before," he says. "We were able to make a living at it for two or three years. I didn't like some of the shit you had to put up with. All in all, it was all right."

Darren Blase, co-owner of Shake It Records, says he liked the Ass Ponies because "they didn't have anything to prove. They were from Ohio. How many bands are from New York? Not that many. Every New York band is from somewhere else. Great bands don't come from Manhattan." The Ass Ponies released their final record in 2001 on an independent label. They played a couple of local shows in 2015 but otherwise have been dormant.

Cleaver grew up north of Cincinnati in Fort Ancient and moved to Cincinnati to study at the University of Cincinnati. He started writing songs as a kid and thought he should learn to play an instrument, so he taught himself guitar. "I figure if I write songs, I should probably try to learn how to play something to say 'here it is.'" Cleaver has seen the Cincinnati scene morph since he started out in the late seventies. "Back then, there was no place to play and the bands were all cover bands," he explains. "We would just sneak into a classroom at University of Cincinnati and have a show. I don't know if you could do that anymore. But we used to do that quite often. We'd go into a classroom and invite some people. We never got kicked out. It was kind of amazing."

In 2001 Cleaver met Walker, who changed his life. "I had a solo show to play and I'm not fond of playing by myself," he says. "I was nervous, and Lisa said, 'I'll play with you,' and that's how Wussy got started." It was Walker's first band, and she added female vocals against the male vocals of Cleaver, former Ass Ponys member Erhardt, drummer Joe Klug, and bassist Mark Messerly.

Wussy's sound could be described as countrified classic rock and punk (they've covered the Who's "Teenage Wasteland" but also Joy Division's "Ceremony"), alongside the additions of lugubrious vibraphone and harmonica. Walker's voice brings raw emotion to their songs, something that was lacking in the Ass Ponys. Needless to say, to see Wussy live is a treat (especially for the flashy pants Messerly is known to wear onstage).

"Wussy—that's a Cincinnati band," Mike Montgomery says. "Is it Cincinnati that makes Chuck Cleaver weird, or is it Chuck Cleaver making Cincinnati weird? Socially, I don't know what came first: the town or the weirdos that just happen to live in that town. A weirdo like Chuck Cleaver—he could live in any little town. Don't call him a weirdo in your book. He's a real nice guy."

I mention to Cleaver that Montgomery referred to him as a "weirdo" and he chortles. "I think all musicians are weird to a certain extent," he says. "There is a certain misfit aspect to being any kind of artist—a writer, a musician, a painter. We're the ones who don't necessarily fit in. I can attest to the fact that we are weirdos. It's a good thing. I've always considered it normal to be weird. You better be happy with it, because you're sure as fuck stuck with it. We think we write really normal songs, but other people have told us we don't. People for the most part have been really nice to us. And the ones who haven't—fuck 'em." The band is content to "write what they know." "I guess we could write songs about fairies and gnomes and shit," he says. "We will now. I can't imagine not writing about what you know."

Since 2005 the group has released either a full-length album or an EP every two years, starting with 2005's *Funeral Dress*. "That's how we normally do it: we make a record, we tour on it, and then we take some time off, and then we just do it again," Cleaver says. "We're very particular editors, and we try not to let too much suck get through. If somebody writes something that's not particularly good, there will usually be at least somebody, if not more than one person, who jumps on it and says, 'this is kind of shitty.' They're all easy and good to work with." When they're not touring, the players hold down day jobs to make ends meet. However, they do make some money playing shows. Cleaver acknowledges how there is "no money in it anymore unless you're some kind of superstar." He says people don't buy physical albums, and it's expensive to press vinyl because not many plants exist today. "When you make a record, you have to wait so ungodly long for it, you almost forget you even did it," he says. But Walker is quick to point out that they have been making more money than before, so things are on the upswing. "We do okay every time we go out," Cleaver says. "We are one of those slow-burn bands that if we live long enough, we actually may make some money at it. That's not why we're in it. Money is a bonus."

I ask them what their goal was in starting Wussy, and Cleaver bursts out laughing. "We're not very goal-oriented," he says. "We just like making records. We're very fortunate to have Shake It as our label. They let us make records. And that's just about as great a thing as you can ask for. It's just something that we do. I can't imagine not doing it. I'm guessing there will be a time when we don't, but I don't see that happening anytime soon."

He thinks Cincinnati imbues a strong DIY scene now, with house shows, unlike in the nineties, when he says "there was a big pop-rock kind of movement." "It tends to be a pretty friendly scene, or at least how I've experienced it," he says. "I think right now there's about as many good to great bands around here than has ever been around here. I'm very proud to be from here. There's just so much different stuff going on right now that's worth a damn here. It's cool to be here." He's not sure why these bands form in Ohio, but he doesn't think it's from boredom. "I don't know if it's any more boring than anywhere else," he says. "It's the individual's fault if they're bored. Since the advent of the internet, it's changed a lot being from Cincinnati," he says. "It used to be the kiss of death. It was the middle of nowhere. Now with the internet, you really can be from anywhere."

Despite Cleaver's seasoned veteran status, he's not intimidated by a younger, less experienced band like Walk the Moon. "They're nice guys and I'm happy for anybody who makes it out of here." He tells a story how he randomly ran into the group at the Grand Canyon. "We were at a fairly remote area of the Grand Canyon, sitting on a bench, and we looked up and said, 'Hey, isn't that one of the guys from Walk the Moon?' He's our practice space neighbor and we saw him in the middle of nowhere. And he was as surprised as we were. People are getting out and touring a lot more than I've previously noticed, at least." It appears that Wussy will just keep recording music and touring and not expecting Walk the Moon–type fame to befall them. And they're good with that. "We've seen each other through break-ups and weirdness and death and birth," Cleaver says. "Everybody is still here. We're best friends. It's a good relationship."

## FOXY SHAZAM

*We don't have enough music industry in Cincinnati or anywhere else in Ohio. You gotta hit the road.*

—Sky White

During an unusually warm January afternoon, the bushy-bearded Sky White and I stroll through Over-the-Rhine, an up-and-coming neighborhood in Cincinnati (the city's idea of Brooklyn). In the course of an hour it becomes clear to me that Sky White is very famous. On two separate occasions, two people with professional cameras stop Sky and ask to take a photo of him (not with him). Both times he obliges, and he flashes them a goofy grin. He says this obsequious behavior happens all the time, and people either recognize him as the keyboardist of glam-rock outfit Foxy Shazam or for his nascent tea company, Wendigo Tea. Since Foxy shut down in 2015, he has quit touring to become a tea entrepreneur. But in 2004, before that occurred, at the age of seventeen, White joined the fledgling six-piece group, led by the Freddie Mercury surrogate Eric Nally. (You might recognize Nally from the 2015 music video for Macklemore's song "Downtown.") The first question I ask White is why so many bands have come from Ohio. He says, "Being a starving artist is important for a lot of people," and those who are raised in a working-class environment need a creative outlet to escape normal life. It's cheap to live in a place like Cincinnati, he says. "How much is the worst apartment in LA? Thousands of dollars? The worst apartment here is a couple hundred bucks."

"We're within a day's drive of so many cities," he continues. "Say you lived in Texas—you're a day's drive within a couple of cities. Say you're trying to start touring—Ohio is about as good as you can get in being able to hit the road." And hit the road the band did, racking up two hundred to three hundred shows a year, because that's one of the only ways they could make money. "It took Foxy five years before we made enough," he says. At one point the stress of doing so many shows caused a tour manager to have a mental breakdown. As Sky tells it, the band noticed the manager talking to a trash can and overheard him trying to book hotels in cities they weren't even playing. Then one day the manager took off with their money and passports. A few weeks later they tracked him down at an Ohio hospital. The manager didn't remember how he got there. "It was horrible, but I loved it," White confesses. "It was dark, and it was weird. Some people have it in them; some don't. But if you don't, don't go on tour."

White is glad he didn't write a tour diary, because he would've written things like "Didn't sleep." "Our last record was called *Gonzo* because we were losing our minds," he says. "If you listen to it, it sounds like we're losing our minds." White says touring was fun—at times—but he missed the familiarity of home. "The travel wears on you and so does missing your friends," he says.

> You have one of those days where you want to go to your favorite restaurant or get some carry-out and sit on the couch, but you can't do that for two and a half months. You have to sleep in a moving van, and then get on an airplane, and then haul gear, and then play a show somewhere super jet-lagged. Then you have a meet and greet and then an acoustic performance, and you sleep for three hours and wake up in another city and have a radio show you have to go do. And you have to sound excited even though you're super exhausted. All of those things are fun, but when you keep tying them on to each other, you're like a zombie rolling through it.

The "fun" began in 2005 with the release of their first full-length, *The Flamingo Trigger*, which they self-released. "When Foxy started, we didn't get paid hardly anything," he says. "That's how we got most of our shows—we said we wouldn't get paid and we'd bring hundreds of people and offered to open for big bands." They played at the now-defunct Mad Hatter in Covington, Kentucky. "They were packed, crazy shows, and we'd open every rock show we could there." (It's worth noting that during one of their performances there, Nally ate a lit cigarette while performing. It's those kind of antics that drew people to their shows.)

Next came the 2008 record *Introducing Foxy Shazam*, followed by their 2010 major label debut, on Sire (owned by Warner Bros. Music Group), which was self-titled. "We were on multiple major labels," White says.

> All of that was great and bad. Everybody who worked at the labels, we liked working with them, but it's the fact you're working in a giant, stupid machine. When we were signed to Warner Brothers, it would take months to get records. But if it was us doing it, we could get it in a couple of weeks. Stuff would show up at the wrong time. Someone would spend tens of thousands of dollars on a thing we didn't need. That comes out of our money. Everybody we met with were lovers of music and were in it because they care about artists and music. It was a weird situation what we went through.

There's a definite benefit on being on a major, especially if you're trying to tour internationally and if you're trying to reach as many people as humanly possible. If you need something to happen, they can find a way to make it happen. When you're just you, it's hard. If we were self-releasing things and touring and booking everything ourselves, Foxy would not have been able to do two hundred to three hundred shows a year.

A week before their album *Foxy Shazam* was released, the label got sold, which threw everything into disarray. "The people we were talking to before our record came out weren't even working there anymore," White says. "We would need records, and there wasn't anybody there. Somebody from the label owned us money, and there wasn't somebody there to write us a check. If the exact people were there when we got signed, I think our experience would've been a little different. I don't want to complain, because all of those people were great. That whole situation was confusing and weird, and on the outside looking in it looked like a poorly run business."

Foxy braved the major label trajectory again with 2012's *The Church of Rock and Roll*, distributed by IRS, a subsidiary of Capitol. The record charted at 24 on Billboard's US alternative music chart and peaked at 115 on Billboard's 200 chart. Justin Hawkins, the lead singer of the similar glam-rock group the Darkness, produced the record. The song "I Like It" reached number 8 on Billboard's US rock songs chart. Needless to say, it was Foxy's biggest album to date. In a circuitous way, in 2014 they went back to self-releasing, on the losing-their-minds record *Gonzo*, which was produced by Steve Albini in Chicago. "Our last record, we made the most money being self-released," White says.

As a Cincy native, White has seen the music scene progress. "One of the big things I think Cincinnati has going on right now is there's this massive correlation between drinking culture and how much bands are getting paid," he says. "Because places bands play serve booze, the more people who drink there, the more the bands are capable of getting paid. In one way there's this sweet spot where bands can make enough money to be able to commit enough to their craft and get good enough to be a professional at it. But if it's paying so much here, there's less incentive to travel. We don't have enough music industry in Cincinnati or anywhere else in Ohio. You gotta hit the road."

When the band adjourned, it enabled White and everybody else to pursue solo endeavors. "We see each other all the time," White says. "Everybody still plays. I can't see us never playing again. I don't know if we'll ever do the two hundred to three hundred shows around the world, though." During White's world travels, he encountered different kinds of tea and has since spun it into an enviable locally based business called Wendigo Tea. (All of his company's teas are named after mythical monsters, such as Bigfoot and Nessy.) He slings the teas at various restaurants and bars around the city and has robust online sales. "I feel like I need Wendigo to have its full potential and let it do its thing in the universe before I can get back into pursuing music," he says. "I'm trying not to make money from playing piano. I'm trying to not have money touch music at all."

## THE GREENHORNES

*I took my guitar off and threw it at him like a spear, like I was trying to send it right through his chest.*

—Brian Olive

The early 2000s ushered in a revisionist interpretation of 1960s garage-rock and garage-punk genres. The White Stripes and the Black Keys tapped into that sound as duos. Cincinnati's the Greenhornes, a five-piece act, sounded blues-rocky but also not. Brian Olive grew up in Bright, Indiana, thirty minutes from Cincinnati. He and high school friend Patrick Keeler created the band Us and Them in school. They graduated and went their separate ways but met up in Cincinnati and formed the Greenhornes in 1996 with guitarist Craig Fox, bassist Jack Lawrence, organist Jared McKinney, Keeler on drums, and Olive on guitar. "We didn't even think about—we just did it," Olive says about wanting to be in a band. "I don't think it's a conscious effort. One day we're like, let's have a band. This is the natural thing to do. In high school it was out of boredom, because we were out in the sticks. There was nothing to do. We turned my basement at my mom's house into a club. We had shows there every weekend."

The group released their first record in 1999, *Gun for You*, which delivered their throwback sound. John Curley engineered it at Ultrasuede. "We were influenced by everything around us," Olive says. "We got our inspiration from playing our records. We'd go to thrift stores and get all the old records we could find—British invasion, old R&B. There was nobody around Cincinnati like us that I can think of. As we started going out of town, playing Cleveland and Detroit, we started finding other people doing that kind of thing." Olive launches into one of the most unusual theories on how everything is connected to Ohio. "There's electromagnetic lines that run through the earth, underground. It's a grid or circuit plate that runs in different places. So one ley line carries a certain energy and could travel anywhere. It could be one from Cincinnati to Tucson, Arizona, so it'd create a similar energy in that the people there could be having similar sorts of inspirations or feelings and be tuned in to something. We can't see them, so nobody's traced them all." His theory is far-fetched but it could be valid. What if that energy is what makes Ohio bands so special? Huh.

Besides stints in Detroit and London, Olive has lived in Cincy for most of his adult life, in the Northside neighborhood, which is a rock and roll microcosm. It's near his recording studio, where he produces solo works and collaborates with local bands. Walking down the street in Northside, you're confronted with people smoking and wearing leather jackets. Vegan restaurants dot Spring Grove and Hamilton Avenues, alongside the residence of one of the best record stores in the region, Shake It. Northside characterizes its rock roots every July in hosting the Northside Rock 'N Roll Carnival. Olive, like everybody else in Northside, looks the part of rock musician, down to the shaggy hair and sideburns. "Northside is the best," he says. "It's like living in a small town that has rock clubs every few places."

Olive champions Cincinnati's eclectic music scene and thinks its geography near the US South and the East adds to the scene. "Every city has people doing different things and different influences, but in Cincinnati you could never tell what people were going to come out with." He thinks Cincinnatians have a more positive attitude today than they did when he first started out. "Cincinnati had a stigma attached to it, as far as the rest of country was concerned," he says. "We'd be on tour and somebody would say, 'Where are you from?' Either they'd never heard of it or they'd immediately say, 'Isn't that where [Robert] Mapplethorpe wasn't allowed to do his [photography]? Isn't that where they gave Larry Flynt all that trouble?' Now people don't have that [impression]. It's like any other town."

In 2001 the Greenhornes released their sophomore record, self-titled. It was around this time that Olive and Keeler stopped getting along, which led to an almost deadly melee on tour. It also was the impetus for Olive's departing the band, right before they had their biggest spurt of success. Olive tells the story of the explosive incident in its entirety:

> Patrick and I started really not seeing eye to eye on anything. After a few years, there was a slight blowup in Atlanta, where we got into it in the back room of the club. I don't remember why. There probably was no reason. It's called magnetic repulsion when you take two magnets and spin one one way, and if you spin them around, they push against each other. You don't really know why, but you're just repulsed. I remember David Cross was at that show in Atlanta and we were having a great time. We were fans of his and were hanging out, and I was thinking what a shit night to get into a brawl in a back room. We tore the place to pieces. We tore each other to pieces. We were all beat up. After that, it was just bad. The air in the van was so thick with tension that everyone was mad all the time.

> It finally came to a head in St. Louis at this place called the Creepy Crawl. I knew I had to leave, but I was trying to stick with it and figure out a way around all the trouble. But that night somebody had told me not to sing on a song that I always sang on, and they were doing it just to mess with me. I retaliated—this was a pretty childish way of doing it, but that was the style at the time. I strummed my guitar with the strings open during the entire song and I could feel this awful energy, and I knew I was making Patrick mad, and that's what I wanted to do. At the end of the song I turned around

to look at him and he had his snare drum, getting ready to pitch it at me, and I took my guitar off and threw it at him like a spear, like I was trying to send it right through his chest. He threw the drum; I ducked. I threw the guitar; he ducked. He jumped over the set and we started punching each other and ended up rolling off the stage. We were trying to kill each other! The last thing I remember was taking the microphone that was still plugged into the PA and I was hitting him in the head with it. You could hear it reverberating through the whole club—*thud, thud*. And they pulled us off of each other and I took off. I got on a bus and came home and was like, I'm out of this band.

Telstar Records released the Greenhornes' *Dual Mono* in 2002, featuring the song "There Is an End," which gained adequate screen time when it was used in the Bill Murray vehicle *Broken Flowers*, directed by Akronite Jim Jarmusch. "I really liked the *Dual Mono* songs that we were working on," Olive says. "I was looking forward to recording it. But when you get to be fighting with somebody like that, you can't do it."

The Greenhornes released only one more full-length album, 2010's *Four Stars*, distributed by Jack White's Third Man Records. Olive left the group and didn't look back. He joined the Detroit- and Ohio-based Soledad Brothers—"Jack White wants to believe he invented the two-piece rock duo with guitar and drums, but the Soledad Brothers were like that before I joined the band, before the White Stripes existed"—and has released several solo albums, including 2017's *Living on Top*. "I did whatever I felt like doing—I always do that—but I did it even more this time, and I'm glad I did, because I love the way it turned out," Olive says about the album.

In 2012 Olive won a Grammy for playing on the Dan Auerbach–produced Dr. John record *Locked Down*. The idea germinated at Riverbend Music Center in 2010, when the Black Keys played a show there. Olive and Auerbach were friends, and Auerbach invited Olive backstage. "We were standing there and hanging out in this sand-beach area, and Dan's like, 'I think I'm going to produce the next Dr. John album. Do you want to play on it?' Four months later I got a message from Dan's management: 'Can you come down to Nashville and do this?' I said, 'Let's do it.'" Olive didn't win one of the nice Grammy statues like Auerbach did. Apparently you have to pay for the statue, so Olive accepted a piece of paper instead.

As for Olive's relationship with Keeler, it didn't mend. "I saw him in Nashville when I working on that Dr. John record with Dan," he says. "Dan said, 'You should talk to Patrick. He misses you. He wants to be friends again.' I said, 'I don't trust that guy. There's too many things. I don't want to get near him.' I did talk to him that night just so the vibe was not too awkward in the room. I said hello, but it wasn't nice to talk to him at all." However, Olive is copacetic with Jack Lawrence, who went on to play in White's Dead Weather and the Raconteurs. "Jack—he always went along with Patrick on things, so that made it difficult to stay friends with him. But we have made up. I've always been tight with Craig, and I'm close friends with Jared." Keeler, on the other hand, now plays drums in the Afghan Whigs.

Olive made a conscious choice to settle in Cincinnati, but I wonder if a musician needs to leave their hometown in order to find success, like what the Black Keys did in moving to Nashville. "I think Auerbach moved his studio to Nashville on Patrick Keeler's recommendation," Olive says, "Maybe they like the weather better there. I know I do."

I ask Olive how the music industry has changed from when he stated out in the nineties, and he thinks it's more challenging today to make it as a musician. "The funny thing is, we started the Greenhornes in ninety-six, and at that time the music business was essentially the same since the sixties: you work hard to get a record contract and hope for the best. Right in the middle of everything that I was working on is when the digital stuff came in and took over. It was hard enough as it was, and then the digital takeover just made it ten thousand times harder. It doesn't mean you can't do it, but you gotta find your way around that."

## HEARTLESS BASTARDS

*In Ohio I feel like if you've got some good solid music going, it'll stand
out. Sometimes in these bigger scenes you can get lost in the shuffle.*

—Erika Wennerstrom

"Heartless Bastards are an Austin band with Cincinnati roots, and
they're comfortable with that," Lisa Walker of Wussy says. The four-
piece Bastards abdicated Cincinnati in 2007 for Austin, Texas, yet
they still identify with their hometown and play there at least once
a year. (Lead singer and founding member Erika Wennerstrom still
rocks a phone number with a 513 area code.)

"Austin's music scene is huge," Wennerstrom says. "Most people
aren't from Austin who live in Austin. People come here and visit
and like it and end up moving. Or maybe they move to grow their
music career. I feel like when you talk about an Ohio music scene,
the majority of the people that are in that music scene are from Ohio.
It's just different." She thinks there are about forty thousand active
musicians living and working in Austin. "When I think about that
many musicians, you can really get lost in the shuffle. In Ohio I feel
like if you've got some good solid music going, it'll stand out. Sometimes in these bigger scenes you can get lost in the shuffle."

Wennerstrom didn't move to Austin just because she liked it. "I
didn't move to Austin because I thought it would bring me more
success," she says. She relocated after a ten-year romantic relationship ended; she needed a new start. "I had a support system here."

Becoming a successful musician doesn't necessarily involve living
in a major music city like Austin. "I think some people have luck, but
I think the majority of people—and even very successful people—
work very hard and they take chances and they take risks, and I
think no matter where you're from—when you take those chances
and those risks, things are more likely to be fruitful. When things
don't happen for them or they realize how much work is involved
in it, they might shy away. But I think that you can do that living in
Ohio or wherever you live."

In the nineties Wennerstrom came of age in her hometown of Dayton, where she played in an all-girl band named Shesus, featuring former Brainiac member Michelle Bodine. Wennerstrom liked to sing from a young age, and she got into rock and roll in high school. "I got really into writing songs when I turned eighteen," she says. "I was an adult, and I was like, if this is truly what I want to do with my life I should probably get on it." Former Guided by Voices bassist Jim Greer used to see her at parties in Dayton and says, "She was so shy. She was the girl with the acoustic guitar. After I moved away from Dayton, I heard them and I was surprised: Heartless Bastards? Who's that? Erika? That's Erika? She was so shy back then that I never knew she had such a big voice. I wouldn't expect that voice to come out of her."

The Bastards formed in 2003 in Cincinnati with fellow Daytonian Dave Colvin, along with Adam McAllister and Michael Weinel. Between bartending gigs, Wennerstrom worked on writing songs, and in 2004 she and the guys signed to former Black Keys label Fat Possum Records, a blues-oriented label. As far as she knows, she was the first woman to be signed to them. Pat Carney recommended her to Fat Possum. The two worked on some demos together, but an album "didn't pan out," she says. Fat Possum released the Bastards' debut album, *Stairs and Elevators*, in 2005. It's worth noting that 2005 also saw the debut of Foxy Shazam's first record and the National's *Alligator*. The label released two more Heartless Bastards records: 2006's *All This Time* and their first charting record, *The Mountain*, in 2009 (by this time the group was based in Austin). The success of those albums garnered them prime slots at Lollapalooza and allowed the NBC television show *Friday Night Lights* to license a couple of their songs. Wennerstrom's voice can best be described as a baritone blues woman—she could lay waste to any male blues artist. For their 2012 record, *Arrow*, the band switched to Partisan Records, and that record became their highest-charting record, reaching number seventy-eight on the Billboard chart. After 2015's *Restless Ones* the band decided to take a pause. "I didn't even realize how much of a break I

needed until it came up," she says. "It was a big weight lifted. Sometimes I don't know how to stop. I don't mean that the band's ending.
I'm always moving. I'm always doing something. I ended up finding
a huge amount of inspiration from that—just giving myself some
space. I'm really driven and excited about what I'm doing right now."

What she's currently doing is solo material. In late 2016 and 2017
she played a few shows without the backing of the Bastards. "I created a band and at times the lineups have changed," she says. "Everybody's added something to it. We've been a great team. If people
hadn't wanted a break, maybe this would've been the next Heartless
Bastards album. I think right now it's nice. I'm just worrying about
myself." Wennerstrom says she didn't used to think of herself as a
role model, but she's noticed that her heart-on-the-sleeve approach
has affected lives. "I think I've always just put one foot in front of
the other, and I hadn't stopped to look back to where I've gotten in
my life, and the last few years I've really stopped and thought about
it and appreciated it and listened to people who had told me that I
inspired them," she says. "I didn't comprehend what some people
were getting out of it. I think it's what drives me, because it's not just
me writing these songs. I don't feel like I'm as self-involved in what
I'm doing now. I'm writing from the heart, but I think what drives
me more now is that somebody else might get something out of it
versus just my own catharsis."

The name Heartless Bastards emerged from Wennerstrom's
thinking she had to be tough to survive. "The more vulnerable you
are is actually the tougher you are, because you're allowing yourself
to be open to the world despite whatever you get back," she says.
"I think it's tougher to be vulnerable. I am tough, but in a different
way." Since starting out during the dawn of the digital age, releasing
records has transmuted for the Bastards. "The landscape changes
so fast these days that every time I release a record it's a completely
different industry," she says. "I'm certainly glad I've gotten to where
I've gotten. I'm sure that from what experience I've already had, I
have some advantage over a new artist. It's still such a learning pro-

cess for everybody I work with. I never feel like I have it completely down, and that's okay. I can tell you the things that used to help me financially aren't the same things now. I'm certainly not surviving much on record sales. But I'm grateful I'm getting by."

The website 45rpmrecords.com catalogs most of the record labels that existed in the Tri-state—Ohio, Indiana, and Kentucky—and West Virginia between the fifties and seventies. Ohio ran an astounding thousand labels, whereas Kentucky and Indiana had maybe two hundred each. Some of the Ohio labels put out only one 45 or 78; other labels put out fifty records. Click on a label and the site lists the artist, song, year, genre, and label address. For instance, Fraternity Records in Cincy dropped almost three hundred recordings from 1954 through 1959. Darren Blase, co-owner of Cincinnati's Northside record store and label Shake It Records, sees the labels—and a once-large number of vinyl-pressing plants—as reasons why so much great music has stemmed from the Buckeye State. "When I was a freshman in high school, I was at Everybody's Records and I bought a Little Willie John [record], and I flip it over and see 'King Records, Cincinnati, Ohio' [written on it.] What the hell? At that age you naturally assume every record comes from LA or New York and that's it. It's that impression. That's why there are so many Ohio records."

At the height of Ohio record labels, pressing plants were also ubiquitous around Cincinnati and everywhere else. "People could open a phone book and there was a pressing plant in their town," Blase says. When he started out, it took him less time to cut a record than it does today. He'd mail off the LP and receive the finished copies days later in the mail. "It took nine days to make a record, but now it takes seven months," he says. "Back then you could walk into QCA on Spring Grove Avenue [in Northside] and beginning to end have a record done." (QCA is a full-service place for recording and pressing a record.)

The Ohio labels didn't just feature Ohio artists; in fact, Blase says 95 percent of Cincinnati-based King Records' musicians were not from the metropolitan area, but Fraternity Records released albums from locals like Dale Wright. Jess Hirbe and Doc Kalmus formed the Shake It label in 1978. Blase took over ownership of the label in 1992, and he and his brother opened the brick-and-mortar haunt in 1999. "We always put our address on our releases, because people don't even put their address on a record," Blase says. "You don't know where they're from. For me, that was such a huge part of buying records."

In 2010 *Rolling Stone* named Shake It one of the best record stores in the country.[2] Blase's store stocks around twenty-five thousand vinyl titles and fifteen thousand CD titles (a combination of mainstream and independent), alongside books, DVDs, clothing, and novelties. It's one of the last independently owned record stores in the city; the label distributed Wussy's first record, in 2005. They also issue albums from national acts, not just local ones. In 2016 they inherited twenty thousand records from a Boston collector. Those types of collections are gold for Blase.

Blase himself owns thousands of Ohio records alone. "I still have my searches saved on eBay, and fifteen things will pop up that I've never heard of or seen," he says. "I didn't know that record existed. There's so much of this it's crazy." One of his favorite obscure Ohio musicians is Mad Lydia, probably the weirdest Ohio artist he owns. "Lydia and Cincinnati Joe were this kind of Stevie Nicks meets Sly Stone kind of thing," he says. "It's this wild, psychedelic freak-out hippie music, but most of the songs are about how evil her mother is." Another one of his favorites is Gibson Bros from Columbus. "They're like a country Velvet Underground," he says. "They were a clusterfuck of noise and twang and yelping. I didn't know if I liked it. But it left an impression with me. The record *Big Pine Boogie* [released on Columbus label OKra Records in 1987] I've listened to more than any Ohio band, and it's the record I have yet to figure out. I don't know if it's a complete piece of shit or if it's pure genius." He thinks

Indiana native Lonnie Mack is the one who really epitomizes the Cincinnati Sound. "He's that perfect combination of soul, country, R&B, and early rock and roll. It's melded into one thing. When you look at Cincinnati on the map, it makes total sense."

Blase understands why Cincinnati has been a nucleus for musicians for so long. Rent is low, which makes it easier for working-class musicians to get by doing what they want. "Music is a release, and that's why great music comes from working-class people—at least the music I like listening to," he says. "It's got soul and means something. It's why [McDonald's] tested the McRib in Ohio—because it's middle America." The so-called Cincinnati Sound is more "all over the place" in the contemporary era than it was in the 1950s or 1970s. However, Blase misses the good old days of specialized analog recordings. "Sadly, people have become more of a sponge," he says. "All of the influences that filtered through their internet cable end up balancing out or drowning out local influences. Now with [the software] GarageBand, the things I like about old-time vernacular music don't really exist anymore." But at least he has thousands of Ohio records to hold on to.

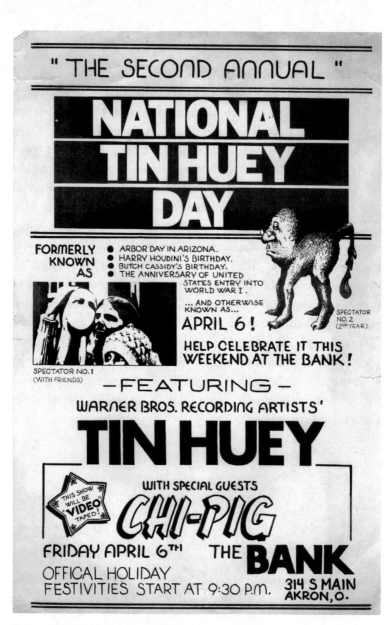

**Figure 1.** Tin Huey and Chi-Pig concert promo poster for a show at the Bank, Akron, Ohio, April 1979. *Photo provided by the "Akron Sound" Museum.*

**Figure 2.** Akron band the Waitresses pose for a press photo, circa early 1980s. *Left to right*: Billy Ficca, Dan Klayman, Mars Williams, Chris Butler, Dave Hofstra, Patty Donahue, Ariel Winter. *Photo provided by the "Akron Sound" Museum.*

**Figure 3.** Chi-Pig, October 1978. *Left to right*: Susan Schmidt Horning, Richard Roberts, Debbie Smith. *Photo credit: Anastasia Pantsios.*

**Figure 4.** Facing: Chrissie Hynde at Akron Civic Theatre, 2000.
*Photo credit: Janet Macoska.*

**Figure 5.** Above: Devo and the Black Keys hang out at a show at the Akron
Civic Theatre, 2008. *Back left to right*: Bob Mothersbaugh, Jerry Casale, Mark
Mothersbaugh, Neil Taylor, Bob Casale. *Front*: Patrick Carney and Dan
Auerbach. *Photo credit: Janet Macoska.*

**Figure 6.** Devo performs at the Agora Theatre, Cleveland, October 1978. *Photo credit: Anastasia Pantsios.*

**Figure 7.** Erika Wennerstrom of Heartless Bastards performs in concert, 2016.
*Photo credit: Kendall Bailey Atwater.*

**Figure 8.** Kelley Deal and Mike Montgomery play at the Northside Rock 'N Roll Carnival, Cincinnati, July 3, 2015. *Photo credit: Garin Pirnia.*

**Figure 9.** Facing: Sky White of Foxy Shazam poses on the streets of Over-the-Rhine, Cincinnati, January 2017. *Photo credit: Garin Pirnia.*

**Figure 10.** Facing: Jane Scott and David Bowie backstage at Blossom Music Center, Cuyahoga Falls, Ohio, 1999. *Photo credit: Janet Macoska.*

**Figure 11.** Above: David Spero with the Eagles, 1994. *Left to right*: Glenn Frey, Joe Walsh, Timothy B. Schmit, Peter Lopez (Glenn Frey's manager), David Spero. *Photo credit: Ellen Spero.*

**Figure 12.** Trent Reznor of Nine Inch Nails performs at Lollapalooza, Blossom Music Center, Cuyahoga Falls, Ohio, 1991. *Photo credit: Anastasia Pantsios.*

**Figure 13.** Richard Patrick of Filter performs, circa 1990s.
*Photo credit: Anastasia Pantsios.*

**Figure 14.** System 56 playing the Phantasy Theater, Cleveland, 1984.
*Photo credit: Bob Ferrell.*

**Figure 15.** Stiv Bators of the Dead Boys at the Agora Theatre, Cleveland, 1977.
*Photo credit: Janet Macoska.*

# Sinkane *Life & Livin' It*

**Figure 16.** Sinkane album cover, *Life and Livin' It*, 2017.
*Photo credit: Shervin Lainez.*

**Figure 17.** Right: Anyway Records cofounder Bela Koe-Krompecher drinks beside the New Bomb Turks' Eric Davidson at the Union Bar and Grill, Athens, Ohio, circa early 1990s. *Photo credit: Bela Koe-Krompecher.*

**Figure 18.** Below: Eric Davidson of the New Bomb Turks performs in front of a crowd at the Union Bar and Grill, Athens, Ohio, circa early 1990s. Also featured is the New Bomb's Jim Weber. *Photo credit: Bela Koe-Krompecher.*

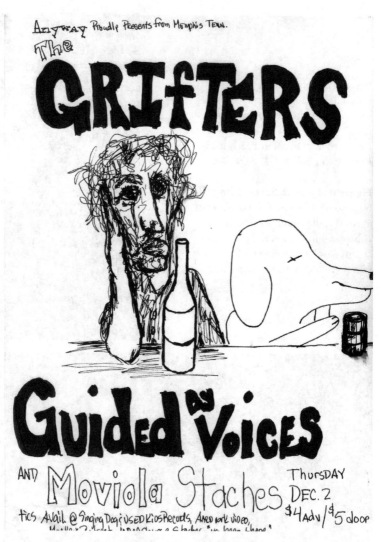

**Figure 19.** Anyway Records poster art for Guided by Voices show at Columbus bar Stache's with the Grifters, 1993. *Poster artist: Bela Koe-Krompecher.*

**Figure 20.** Cleveland band Prisonshake poster art for a show with the New Bomb Turks at Bernies, Columbus, circa 1994. *Poster artist: Bela Koe-Krompecher.*

**Figure 21.** Promo poster for the release of Athens band Appalachian Death Ride's self-titled album on Anyway Records, circa 1995. *Poster artist: Bela Koe-Krompecher.*

**Figure 22.** Guided by Voices lineup in 2016. *Left to right*: Robert Pollard,
Mark Shue, Kevin March, Doug Gillard, Bobby Bare Jr. *Photo credit:
Matt Davis.*

**Figure 23.** The author (Garin Pirnia, *left*) with R. Ring and the Breeders' Kelley Deal, April 2012. *Photo credit: Mike Montgomery.*

**Figure 24.** Facing top: The Terrifying Experience plays at Therapy Cafe, Dayton, January 2017. *Left to right*: Mitch Mitchell, El Beano, Luis Lerma. *Photo credit: Garin Pirnia.*

**Figure 25.** Facing bottom: Team Void plays at Therapy Cafe, Dayton, January 2017. *Left to right*: El Beano (on bass), Luis Lerma (guitar), Mitch Mitchell (drums). A few months after this photo was taken, Mitchell departed ways with the band and the Lermas left the Terrifying Experience. *Photo credit: Garin Pirnia.*

**Figure 26.** Motel Beds play CMJ Music Marathon, New York City, 2012. *Left to right*: Darryl Robbins (guitar), Ian Kaplan (drums), Paul John Paslosky (vocals), Tommy Cooper (guitar), Tod Weidner (bass). *Photo credit: Francesca Tamse.*

**Figure 27.** Facing: Flyer announcing Brainiac's show in Los Angeles at Jabberjaw, June 28, 1996. *Poster artist: Nathan Hamill.*

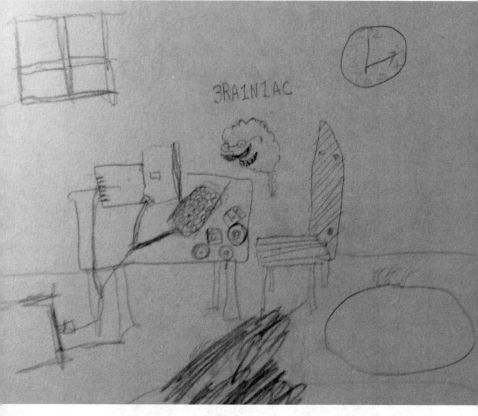

**Figure 28.** Thirteen-year-old Griffin Hamill's drawing of Brainiac, circa 1996. *Artwork by Griffin Hamill.*

**Figure 29.** Facing: The Hamills wearing Brainiac T-shirts on Christmas Day 2016. *Left to right*: Nathan Hamill, Mark Hamill (sitting), and Griffin Hamill. *Photo credit: Griffin Hamill.*

# CLEVELAND

CLEVELAND IS FOUR HOURS NORTH OF CINCINNATI, WHICH lost the bid for the Rock and Roll Hall of Fame and Museum. When the institution opened on the shores of Lake Erie in 1995, it gave the city yet another sobriquet: the Rock Capital of the World. Before then Cleveland's rock status was cemented in 1979 when Ian Hunter—not from Ohio—recorded a song called "Cleveland Rocks"; the Presidents of the United States of America recorded a cover version for *The Drew Carey Show*'s theme song (Carey is a native son). And then came 1984's hilarious film *This Is Spinal Tap*, in which the fictional group Spinal Tap yells to a concert audience, "Hello, Cleveland!" The phrase stuck. Pop culture references aside, a lot has changed for Cleveland since the 1950s, when its population was almost a million—it has since stabilized to around four hundred thousand, making it the second-largest city in Ohio. The steel and automotive industries receded in the eighties, causing the unemployment rate to balloon to 13.8 percent.

In the twenty-first century, Cleveland's main industries are biomedicine and rock and roll. Garage-rock bands like the Outsiders and the Grasshoppers (featuring the Cars founding member Benjamin

Orr) populated the scene in the 1960s, and the 1970s saw proto-punk groups the Dead Boys, Rocket from the Tombs, the Pagans, and the Electric Eels tear up the scene locally and in New York. Bone Thugs-n-Harmony, Screamin' Jay Hawkins, and Bobby Womack are from the Cleveland area. In the mid-seventies Pere Ubu gutted listeners with their avant-garde underground rock on "30 Seconds over Tokyo." On September 22, 1972, David Bowie brought Ziggy Stardust to town and performed his first show ever in America at Cleveland Music Hall. He enjoyed the town so much, he returned in November and played more shows. Even singer-songwriter Robert Bensick made a statement. In 1975 he recorded his album *French Pictures in London* featuring Cleveland underground musicians, but it took until 2016 for Florida's Smog Veil label to release the once-tabled album. It, too, was weird: acid jazz meets rock.

"Teenagers and creative people with a lot of energy in Ohio in the sixties and seventies didn't have immediate gratification, so they had to make their own fun," David Giffels says. "Robert Christgau made the observation that in Ohio you have basements and garages and barns and places for a band to set up and bash away with no worries. But in New York you don't have the physical rooms. I think a defining song is the Dead Boys' 'Ain't Nothin' to Do' [1977]. It just captures that exact notion of what rock and roll is."

"If you look at our take on things, it's always a little grittier and a little more of an underdog stance," says Annie Zaleski, a Cleveland-based and -bred music critic who was a managing editor for Cleveland's *Alternative Press* magazine. "It's almost like this is going on here, we're going to do our take on it, and we're going to do it better. We're going to do it with more urgency, and we don't care if you like it or not. There's more of an attitude with that stuff. They're not necessarily saying we're going to make it big. In LA everybody is always trying to get ahead. I think in Cleveland a lot of it is, we're going to do the best we can, and if we don't make it, then it's your problem, not our problem."

Eric Davidson of Columbus punk band the New Bomb Turks grew up in Cleveland during the seventies but started attending a lot of concerts in the eighties. "The town was not inviting to original music," he says. "Most bars wanted cover bands or DJs; they didn't want to have new bands play." To him, Cleveland seemed more East Coast than Third Coast (a nickname for the Great Lakes region). "You had intellectual discussions at bars and great college radio, but it's still a working-class town," he says. "It's this love/hate thing with your town that Cleveland's very good at—making fun of itself is almost like a badge of honor. That kind of attitude works well with punk rock, like we're just going to make fun of ourselves. There's a certain kind of sarcasm in the Ohio area that doesn't fly in other parts of the country, a weird mix of Midwest old-world values of hard work and dealing with the cold weather and shut-up-and-deal-with-it mixed with hating all of that, too, but then staying there because it was cheap."

Cleveland is only forty-five minutes from Akron, so the two cities get intertwined. Their close proximity makes it easy for bands to play in both places. Cleveland is within driving distance of other musical cities as well: Detroit is two and a half hours; Chicago is about six hours; Columbus and Pittsburgh are about two hours; and Dayton is only three hours away. "In terms of being able to get your name out there and do some touring, bands from here can do weekend jaunts," Zaleski says.

Punk bands have defined Cleveland's musical landscape, but it's unclear why. Giffels thinks Akron's sound was always artier compared to Cleveland's. "Cleveland always seemed more violent and dark, and I don't know where that came from," he says. "I felt 10 percent more threatened at Cleveland shows than at Akron and Kent shows."

Not all of the Forest City's (possibly named after Cleveland's Forest City baseball team) music was based in punk, though. The Raspberries ("Go All the Way") and Eric Carmen's solo work

("Hungry Eyes," "All by Myself") were embedded in power-pop, which was ubiquitous during the days of classic rock. New Wave or the New Romantic genre bit System 56 and the Exotic Birds in the 1980s. Singer-songwriter Jason Molina recorded under the names Songs: Ohia and Magnolia Electric Co., and Mark Kozelek recorded as the Red House Painters and Sun Kil Moon, releasing the song "Carry Me Ohio." Karen O (Orzolek) and Brian Chase of the art-rock band Yeah Yeah Yeahs met at Oberlin College's conservatory program, moved back to New York, started the band with Nick Zinner, and set the New York music scene ablaze in the early 2000s. In the late eighties and early nineties, trailblazers like Nine Inch Nails (NIN) and Filter morphed Cleveland rock into a hard, industrial sound. Gregg Gillis, aka mashup artist Girl Talk, went to college at Case Western Reserve University and released the EP *Stop Cleveland Hate* in 2004. "All of Ohio cities have a lot of soul," Giffels says. "They have that authenticity of hard times endured."

"You're not going to see a band coming out Cleveland that's going to be shiny, happy, candy-coated music," Zaleski says. "You think of NIN and Filter—it's very much like, we are working to get by, we are working to make ends meet. No one is handing us anything. That's a DIY thing. No one is expecting a big suit to come by and give you a pile of money or a record deal. In Cleveland, people need to make things happen for themselves."

Another factor that influenced local musicians, Giffels thinks, is Ghoulardi (né Ernie Anderson). From 1963 to 1966 he hosted the local TV show *Shock Theater*, which screened horror films and played background garage-rock music. He quit the show and traded in Cleveland's cold winters for the sunny skies of LA. (He also fathered acclaimed filmmaker Paul Thomas Anderson, who directed the weird and wonderful *Boogie Nights*.) "He was just this crack," Giffels says. "He had this weird sense of humor that I see come out in Ohio bands."

Former Cleveland Browns player Josh Cribbs has a saying about Northeast Ohio: "We almost always almost win," a point of view that seeps into music.[1] In June 2016 the region's "almost" identity changed when the Cavs won their first basketball championship ever. It was also the first time any major Cleveland sports team had won a championship in fifty-two years. "The idea of being the outsider is central to rock and roll, and in the sports world we were the outsider for half a century," Giffels says about the victory. "That ironic sense of humor—a lot of that has to do with knowing that every time Charlie Brown goes to kick the football and Lucy pulls it away, you can't come away from that without a strong sense of irony. Every time we're about to win, we're fully aware that something is going to go terribly wrong. There's a Tin Huey song called 'Hump Day.' It's a song about factory life. I think that song captures that whole sense of put your nose down and work, because it's the only way."

### CLOUD NOTHINGS

*There's a huge, long lineage of weird, fucked-up bands coming out of Cleveland. I don't know why that is, but I like it.*

—Dylan Baldi

Cleveland native Dylan Baldi wasn't keen on going to college, so after attending three months of classes at Case Western University, he dropped out of school and formed Cloud Nothings. "Starting a band seemed like a sensible alternative to going to college, even though that's ridiculous," Baldi says. He played in his first band in middle school, and Ohio teenage boredom led him to start recording as Cloud Nothings in his bedroom. "I had to do something or else I'd go crazy," he says, "so I started hanging out in my room a lot with a guitar and writing songs. I think a lot of people in the Midwest I've talked to have similar stories about why they started bands and why they started playing music with friends: so they would have something to do. If you're not twenty-one, you're not going to the bar. When you're in Cleveland, that's about it to do."

He speculates why a lot of people form bands in Ohio: "There's a lot of good music everywhere. But from Ohio and the Midwest, specifically, I think a lot of it stems from not having a goal necessarily with the music you make. If you're on the East Coast, there's New York, and that is where the industry is. Or the West Coast, there's LA. You can have those kinds of spots to reach toward. But if you're in Cleveland, what's the point? So you can do your own thing. A lot of bands historically have done that. A lot of them end up as grimy and weird because of that. I think that has a lot to do with it."

As a youngster he saw his dad's cover band play and thought he could do that, too. In 2009 he recorded and released the *Turning On* EP, and in 2011 came his first full-length record, self-titled, distributed by Carpark Records (all of his subsequent albums were also on Carpark). But in 2012 he got a little heat off *Attack on Memory*, produced by the famed producer/audio engineer/musician Steve Albini, who also worked on records from Ohio bands the Breeders and Foxy Shazam. *Memory* featured his first record with a complete band (current members are drummer Jayson Gerycz, bassist T. J. Duke, and guitarist Chris Brown). The punk-inspired record received oodles of critical acclaim, including the Best New Music stamp from tastemaker music site Pitchfork.com. Baldi's early records sound like Cleveland in that they have the power-pop sensibilities of the Raspberries and the weird art-rock of Pere Ubu and Dead Boys.

"Pere Ubu appealed to me," Baldi says, when he discovered them at Cleveland record store My Mind's Eye. "They were really bizarre and very artsy, but not in a snobby kind of way. There's a huge, long lineage of weird, fucked-up bands coming out of Cleveland. I don't know why that is, but I like it. I'm glad that is Cleveland's reputation." He mentions the Electric Eels and 9 Shocks Terror as other influences. "It's hard-core but it's punk, and it's damaged in a way that only comes from this area." Baldi also checks Ghoulardi as an influence. "My dad loved him. I have a Ghoulardi T-shirt. That was just another aspect of how weird Cleveland is, I guess."

The oddball mentality threads throughout the Cleveland sound, and Baldi considers that one must be a bit odd to want to be in a rock band in the first place—which isn't indicative of being from

Ohio. "I think to be the kind of person who wants to be in a rock band in this age, in this era in time, is weird because rock music is not even popular anymore. You have to be a strange person to be someone who is stoked to get in a van with four smelly people to drive around the country. That's a weird thing to do. Luckily you can transfer that weirdness into something cool."

After *Attack on Memory*—which is available to listen to at the Rock and Roll Hall of Fame Library and Archives in Cleveland—Cloud Nothings released *Here and Nowhere Else* in 2014 and *Life Without Sound* in 2017, a somewhat poppier record than its predecessor. "One of the biggest indie bands to come out of Cleveland is Cloud Nothings," Annie Zaleski contends. "It's been cool to see how they've evolved from a bedroom project to this tight, post-punk band that's a good live band. They've transcended where they come from, but they're loyal to Cleveland. They make sure Cleveland is a stop on the tour, and they've done their best to say, 'We're from Cleveland and we're proud of it.'" Cloud Nothings kicked off their 2017 world tour at the Beachland Ballroom in Cleveland to a sold-out crowd. "It does get a little crazier every time [we play home]," Baldi says. "People are more ready to go wild."

Cloud Nothings spent most of 2017 appearing at big fests like Lollapalooza, the Nelsonville Music Festival in Ohio, and playing gigs in Japan. "It used to be Cleveland was the one place we would play where people stood there and watched us," Baldi says. "What do we have to do to get this place to like us?" He says the Cleveland music scene used to be "fragmented" but is changing for the better. "There was no moving between certain elements of the scene, but now it seems a little more open-minded. I guess it seems everybody supports everything else in a way I didn't notice when I started this band. I feel like the scene has more bands than back then."

I saw Baldi and his band play the Woodward Theater in Cincinnati in 2015 as part of the annual MusicNOW Festival. Will Butler of Arcade Fire opened for them and performed music from his solo record. Baldi told me an anecdote of how Cloud Nothings trolled

Butler just because he's in Arcade Fire: "We kept calling him big, bad Billy Butler. But not when he was around. We drew a picture of a do-rag on his photo in the green room. At one point our drummer was like, 'Oh, big, bad Billy Butler.' And I turned around and he was right there. We blew it. We'll never get to play with Arcade Fire." Whatever it takes to keep your sanity on tour, I guess.

Since Baldi started releasing music in 2009, the music industry has morphed into a volatile monster. He says it used to be he'd post music to his MySpace page and send mp3s to blogs so that other people could discover the songs. "In my mind there was a clear path to what you do, even though it was a weird path," he says. "It was all online. If I had to start a band now, I would be very lost and confused. It does seem different. But I guess that's the nature—everything has changed." For Baldi, change comes with more cachet. Cloud Nothings is one of the more popular bands to break out of Cleveland in the new century, and like so many other Ohio bands, they're doing their thing and continuing Cleveland's pedigree of eldritch rock bands—in a major way.

### DAVID SPERO AND THE EAGLES REUNION

*The next thing we knew the three of them—Don, Glenn, and Joe— were talking, and* Hell Freezes Over *was on the books.*

—David Spero

In 1993 rumblings of an Eagles reunion began in Cleveland. Local talent manager David Spero managed Joe Walsh, who became famous in the late sixties and early seventies as a member of the influential Cleveland rock group the James Gang; Walsh joined the Eagles in 1975. (*Rolling Stone* named him one of the all-time greatest guitarists.) It's well-documented that the Eagles acrimoniously separated in 1980 and swore to reunite only if hell froze over. Hades didn't freeze, but tensions melted enough in 1993 for Walsh and Glenn Frey to open the communication engine. Frey was in Cleveland for a gig and phoned Spero. "I hadn't talked to Glenn since the

Eagles broke up thirteen years earlier," Spero says. The guys agreed to meet at Harvey's BBQ. Frey asked Spero who he was managing.

> I said, "I'm managing Joe."
>
> He says, "You're managing Joe Cocker?"
>
> "I'm managing Joe Walsh."
>
> And he goes, "Yeah, forget him. I've tried to get in touch with him over the years, and I keep being told that he doesn't want anything do with me."
>
> And I said, "That's interesting, Glenn, 'cuz we've tried to get in touch with you over the last couple of years and we were told same thing."
>
> I said to him, "Ya know, if you and Joe played together, you'll be playing much bigger places"—he was playing the [eighteen-hundred-seat] Agora Theatre that night. I said, "The two of you could be doing Eagles stuff and your solo stuff."
>
> And he says, "It's too much water under the bridge." He was having trouble selling tickets for his show at the Agora.
>
> I told him, "Michael Stanley is on the radio here. Let's go over there tomorrow and you guys can hype the show."
>
> He's like, "Why don't we do that."

Stanley, Cleveland's answer to Bruce Springsteen, was a well-regarded heartland musician in the eighties but at the time hosted (and still hosts) an afternoon radio show on WNCX, a classic rock station. During the taping of the radio show, Spero snuck to his car and used his car phone to call Walsh.

> I said to him, "I need you to call Michael Stanley's show. We need to sell some tickets for our show coming up next month, so why don't you get on the air and do an interview?" He goes, "Okay." So I go upstairs and I'm sitting in the studio with Glenn, and the hotline rings. The producer of the show sends Michael a little note that says Joe Walsh is on line two. So Michael looks at me—he knew what was coming up, because I set it up with him. He says, "Glenn, you're never going to guess who is on the phone."
>
> He says, "You're right. Who is it?"
>
> "Joe Walsh."

So Glenn gives me the finger and is just shaking his head. He can't believe I'm doing this. Joe didn't know Glenn was in the studio, and Michael says, "Ya know who is in the studio, Joe? Glenn Frey."

And Glenn was like, "Oh, my God, it was so good to talk to you!" and they went through it all. By the end of phone call, which was live on the air— Michael didn't get involved in the call—they said, "We need to do some stuff together, and, yeah, let's talk when we get back to California."

Once back in LA, Walsh and Frey played a sold-out show together. "By that time it was really a love fest between the two of them," Spero says. Walsh and Frey spent the summer touring together. "Toward the end of the tour, Irving Azoff, Don Henley's manager, called me saying, 'Don Henley wants to sit in and Glenn keeps saying no.' Finally, at one point he did say yes, and the next thing we knew, the three of them—Don, Glenn, and Joe—were talking and *Hell Freezes Over* was on the books." The late seventies Eagles lineup— Walsh, Henley, Frey, Don Felder, and Timothy B. Schmit—reunited for the massive Hell Freezes Over tour in 1994. They released the eponymous live album, which included a few new songs, and it sold nine million copies. Spero says while Walsh was on tour, he liked to superglue hotel furniture to the ceiling. "He was known for that," Spero says. "He did that more than once. He got bored. Hotels used to love when Joe was coming, because they'd give him a room that needed to be renovated; by the time he was done with it, it would get renovated."

Though Spero managed big names like Walsh and Stanley, he was anchored in Cleveland. He got his start on the locally taped *Upbeat*, a syndicated *American Bandstand*–type TV program produced by his dad, Herman Spero. David was also a DJ for the once album-oriented rock (AOR) station WMMS. "I give my dad an awful lot of credit for *Upbeat*, which brought so many acts here between 1964 and 1971," Spero says. "The main reason they came to Cleveland was to do *Upbeat*, because it was on all over the country, and it was a great opportunity for a guy like Tommy James, and the Turtles. They knew they could come here and their next hit was going to be shown on TV right away. It was a huge influence on the entire music market." Spero credits why so many great bands have formed in Northeast Ohio to the city's stellar and wide-reaching top-ten market radio.

"It doesn't have the appeal today like it used to, unfortunately," he says. "I think radio was always so behind the bands from the area, so it was quite easy for them to put out a record and get airplay immediately. And then other cities would always look at what Cleveland was doing. As a result of that, they would start playing the record, too. Pere Ubu—I think they were probably the first ones to come out and really get it done, because of great radio support."

Like the music industry, the management industry has morphed a lot since the 1970s. Spero thinks there are more opportunities for bands to make money today through licensing to video games, TV shows, and commercials, and there are more opportunities on a global scale. But it still isn't what it was in the seventies or even the nineties. "When I started, the first band I ever managed was the Michael Stanley Band," Spero says. "We made a decision from day one that we weren't going to be a local band, even though we were from Cleveland. We really made sure that we didn't play the majority of our shows here in town. We played in other cities and other states and went out to make our mark in other places, so in that case it was a little different."

When Frey passed away in 2016, it was like losing a family member for Spero. He mentions a conversation he had with a friend about all of the great entertainers who died that year. "They were saying something about how all of their idols were gone," he says. "I said, 'They might have been your idols, but they were my friends.'" Spero is a part of rock history, whether he realizes it or not. "I haven't taken time to look back. It's kind of been my life," he says. "I like to say that I've worked for the last thirty-five years but I've never had a job, because I make sure that I always work with good people. If I can't wear the T-shirt, I don't want to be involved with it." But he does acknowledge the impact that the Forest City has had on the world. "David Bowie didn't make it until he made it in Cleveland," he says.

"If it wasn't for Cleveland radio, we most likely wouldn't have the propellant to go further."

FILTER // NINE INCH NAILS

*There was this 'tude coming from so much of Cleveland at this time. Maybe I was a little hard on people, too. I just remember thinking to myself, fuck this.*

—Richard Patrick

Cleveland did not invent industrial music—you can thank England's Throbbing Gristle for being an early progenitor—but in the eighties and nineties, Clevelanders Richard Patrick and Trent Reznor helped give the city one of its most distinguishing sounds. Richard Patrick was born in Massachusetts but moved to Bay Village, Ohio, in 1976, at the age of eight. (His older brother is Robert Patrick, who played the T-1000 in *Terminator 2: Judgment Day*.) Trent Reznor also grew up on the East Coast, in Pennsylvania, and moved to Cleveland after a year in college in the mid-eighties. In high school Patrick had a band called the AKT, which, much to his chagrin, sounded like U2. "A record company had wrote [me] back and said, 'We're not into this. We like the singer's voice but you sound too much like U2.' I had this scorned teenage boy overreaction," Patrick recalls. "I removed my U2 posters off the wall." While hanging out at a record store, a friend walked in and told Patrick his music reminded him of Chicago band Ministry's 1988 industrial record *The Land of Rape and Honey*. "And I'm like, holy fuck," Patrick says. "Overnight I realized how different it was to take synthesizers and samplers and something used by Depeche Mode and Information Society. That's what the Exotic Birds were doing with synthesizers, but wimpy."

Once in the mid-eighties the AKT opened for the Exotic Birds, a synth-pop group in which Reznor played keyboards. (He also played keys for Slam Bamboo, the antithesis of what NIN would be.) So when Patrick and Reznor ran into each other at local audio store Pi Keyboards and Audio, Reznor remembered him. The two started hanging out, right around the time Reznor was shaping Nine Inch Nails' debut record, *Pretty Hate Machine*. Patrick had been influenced by Ministry and also by the Canadian hard-core group Skinny Puppy. "Skinny Puppy was unbelievable," Patrick says. "They were the most unvarnished, terrifying, avant-garde crazy shit we had ever heard." He told Reznor how much he loved industrial music, "and Trent goes, 'I got signed to a record company and I want [you] to go on tour [with me].'" TVT Records released the platinum-selling *Pretty Hate Machine* in 1989. "Trent, he didn't want to be as heavy as Skinny Puppy or as light as Depeche Mode. I wanted to be somewhere between Depeche Mode and Skinny Puppy, and that was what he sent to me when he was playing me *Pretty Hate Machine*." Unfortunately for Patrick, Reznor bought him a pink guitar to play on tour, because pink is in the album's record cover. "I said, 'I don't care. I'm not going to have pink on my body,'" Patrick says. "So I took the guitar home and Sharpee'd the whole thing black. I showed up the next day. There was this roadie named Marco. He goes, 'You took a seventeen-hundred-dollar guitar and you Sharpee'd it black?' I'm like, 'Yeah, fuck you.'"

In 1990 Patrick grabbed his not-so-pink guitar and headed out on tour with Reznor. "When we went on tour, we went full-bore punk rock. People would give us demo tapes and we would crack them in half and throw them back in their faces. We were so arrogant and drunk. It was Gary Oldman in the movie *Sid and Nancy*. I finally understood punk rock. I wanted to punch people in the face. We were so hell-bent on checking out of society. We were just acting out—[does snotty voice] 'I'm not going to fucking brush my teeth because you told me.' Trent and I had that vibe so hard."

Two years on tour led Patrick to move to Los Angeles for a year, but in 1991 he returned to Cleveland to form his own industrial-sounding group, Filter, with Brian Liesegang. However, Patrick couldn't find the right touring musicians. "Sadly, I needed a bigger gene pool," he says. So he went to Chicago and found his gang.

Patrick is a hoot to talk to. He curses a blue streak, he speaks in an unfiltered manner, and occasionally he bursts into name-that-tune songs. In a long story he explained to me Cleveland's punk-rock attitude at that time. "I ran into this kid from the [Cleveland] band Craw. I said, 'Hey, man, I got this record contract from Warner Brothers. I left Nine Inch Nails and I'm doing Filter, and I'm excited to come back to Cleveland and bring my friends with me.'" Patrick says the musician copped a holier-than-thou attitude and called him a "sellout," and sarcastically asked, "What are you going to do—hang out with Martha Quinn?," who was a prominent MTV VJ back then. "We had to sit through ten years of hairspray heavy metal bullshit on MTV and on the radio," Patrick says, "and then overnight, as soon as the new decade started, it was just Nirvana. Jane's Addiction."

> Everybody was just super alternative. And this kid says to me [in a snotty kid voice], "Do you know what I do during the days?"
>
> I said, "What?"
>
> He says, "I wash dishes, because I'm not gonna sell out."
>
> "Wait a minute—you aspire to be an artistic dishwasher?"
>
> He says, "No, but we're not going to fucking sell out and talk to Martha Quinn and try to hawk our record."
>
> "So you're proud of washing dishes?" I asked.
>
> There was this weird punk aspect to this kid. I told him, "You're selling out because you're doing something you don't want to do for money. All I'm doing is making music and talking to people about my music."
>
> There's this attitude from people—they don't see it as an opportunity. In Chicago there was Billy Corgan [of Smashing Pumpkins]. He made it. There was Veruca Salt [best-known for their 1994 hit "Seether"]. They made it. Why? Because they wanted to do it. They'd met every opportunity with a smile.

Patrick recounts another heated encounter with a Cleveland band, this time the hard-core group the Spudmonsters. Patrick auditioned the band's drummer, Eric Matthews, to tour with Filter, but the guy wanted to bring his girlfriend to rehearsals. "I said, 'No, we're just going there to make music. It's not a hang.' He says, 'Well, then I don't know if I can do it.'" Patrick told him, in so many words, to get lost, which didn't sit well with the Spudmonsters' guitar player.

"He heard about it and attacked me at [music venue] the Grog Shop," Patrick says. "It was a little strange at the time when I came back [to Cleveland from LA]. There was this 'tude coming from so much of Cleveland at this time. Maybe I was a little hard on people, too. I just remember thinking to myself, fuck this. I remember a lot of drunken craziness." While recording Filter's debut full-length, *Short Bus*, in Cleveland exurb Rocky River, a twenty-two-year-old Patrick entertained himself in an unusual way. "We'd get under the transportation bridge, under Cleveland, and wander underneath that thing," he says. "There's an access road for communication lines and fiber optics. We would get underneath that and walk around and drink up there."

In May 1995 Reprise Records distributed *Short Bus*. "It was not polished; it was not produced. It was raw and it was angry—and somehow we had drum machines in it." Despite NIN and Filter being filed in the industrial genre, Patrick says Reznor had zero influence on Filter's music. "I drew everything I could from Nirvana, Ministry, and Skinny Puppy," he says. "It wasn't how much influence Trent had on me. Trent was the guy who did it. He was like, 'Fuck it. I got into a studio. I made this record. I got a deal. I spent a lot of time learning how to sing.' That was the only influence: the fact he said, 'This is what I'm doing, here I go. Who's with me?'" Actually, Patrick thinks *he* influenced Reznor.

> When he started *Broken* [his second release and first EP], he even said, "I was influenced by my live band," and that's what I did for NIN. I don't mean to sound like a dick and it's all about me, but I was in Nine Inch Nails and there was a massive change between *Pretty Hate Machine* to *Broken*, and I was the guy saying make it harder, make it cooler, make it tougher, meaner, not lighter. But we didn't want to go too far. We still wanted to get on the radio and have some kind of mass appeal. That was the fine line on that—how far is too much.

The first single—and still one of Filter's most popular songs— "Hey Man, Nice Shot"—crossed that line and caused a vortex of controversy when it was released in 1995. Patrick wrote the song about the shocking 1987 on-air suicide of Pennsylvania treasurer

R. Budd Dwyer, who had been convicted of bribery and awaited sentencing. During a televised press conference, Dwyer took a gun out of an envelope, cocked it to his head, and killed himself. "To me it was like, who does that? We didn't have the internet back then, so when you saw videos like that it was rare. I saw this video and I started writing 'Hey Man, Nice Shot,' and my record company and everybody said, 'Don't say what it's actually about, because people will be turned off.' I said, 'I don't think so.' There's this backlash that was happening from the Reagan years. Everybody was so squeaky clean from the eighties that there was this super-pissed-off arrogance in the nineties."

As Filter's star rose, NIN's trajectory headed into the stratosphere. Reznor's eight-song *Broken* contained the song "Wish," which in 1993 won NIN its first of two Grammy Awards for Best Metal Performance. (In 1996 the song "Happiness Is Slavery" won in the same category.) In 1994 NIN's sophomore full-length, the Grammy-nominated *The Downward Spiral*, gave the world "Closer" and sold more than three million records. Akin to Akron's Mark Mothersbaugh, Reznor became a film composer. He and current NIN bandmate Atticus Ross won an Oscar in 2011 for creating the brooding score to David Fincher's *The Social Network*; they worked with Fincher again and composed music for *The Girl with the Dragon Tattoo*. Even though NIN's enormous purview can be heard in many other rock bands around the world, the Rock and Roll Hall of Fame has twice passed on nominating the band for induction.

In 1997 Patrick headed into the studio and recorded the follow-up to *Short Bus*, *Title of Record*, which Reprise released in August 1999. In November the record spawned the hit song "Take a Picture," based on Patrick's struggles with drug addiction. With its gossamer melodies, it took a 180-degree departure from the hard-rockness of "Hey Man." The best thing the song did was peel back Patrick's screaming vocals to prove what a great singing voice he had (there's still some screaming on the song, though). "'Take a Picture' was the punk-rock answer to the fact that everything had been so goddamn heavy," Patrick says. "We needed a song that was about dealing drugs that sounded like drugs, as opposed to 'let's do drugs and punch people in the face.' You know what I mean? I wanted something that sounded like an opioid, so that was my punk rock. I don't think it went over, because it became a huge pop hit. That's fine. It put my kids through school." Filter's first two albums went platinum, and the third record, 2002's *The Amalgamut*, sold modestly in comparison.

Patrick no longer lives in Cleveland—he settled down in LA in the late nineties. Patrick and Filter (with a rotating list of musicians) still release albums, but the group hasn't bottled the success it had from the mid- to late nineties. However, Patrick notices Filter's sound in other bands. "Sadly, there's been a lot of covers of 'Hey Man' done over the years by folks who I don't think are that cool. When Nickelback covers 'Hey Man,' I don't think it's cool. But I hear a lot of people say Filter had rubbed off on them. Now, maybe now I'm the jaded guy. I don't think that Nickelback have necessarily contributed in the right way. If I had an influence on them, I'm kind of like, ugh."

Patrick sounds equally cynical when we discuss how rock and roll isn't what it used to be. He talks about a time when he was mixing *Short Bus* at an LA recording studio. Patrick was in one booth and a kid named Marshall Mathers, aka Eminem, was in another, rapping the lyrics to what would become *The Marshall Mathers LP*, released in 2000. It not only topped the charts, but it also sold thirty-two million copies worldwide. "That's when I realized rock is in a strange place and it's not coming back. And it didn't," Patrick says. To elaborate, he says the Killers came out and made rock music "nice and sweet," and after 9/11 happened, "No one wanted to be heavy anymore. Everyone wanted church," which led to softer rock bands like Coldplay becoming more necessary. "So much of the music scene has changed," Patrick laments. "I love a lot of it, but there's so much pop music now. Neil Young, with his crazy voice that's not pitch perfect, would have a hard time in today's world. There's a lot of musicians who are not perfect. That's why I like the Black Keys."

That snotty kid from Craw may have been jealous about Patrick hanging out with Martha Quinn; however, he didn't predict in what way MTV would become a boon for Patrick. When then MTV reporter Tina Johnson interviewed Patrick, a relationship sparked, and the couple married in 2006. "Martha Quinn—I would've baked her a cake if I knew what was going to happen," Patrick says.

### JANE SCOTT

*She was always herself.*

—Annie Zaleski

Jane Scott was born in Cleveland in 1919. In 1942, shortly after graduating college, she worked as an advertising secretary for the *Cleveland Press*, spent time in the navy, and then a few days after Alan Freed's seminal Moondog Coronation, one of the first rock concerts, she found a full-time staff job at Cleveland's *Plain Dealer* in 1952, where she would work for the next fifty years. They hired her to cover events like weddings and debutante balls for the society section, a far cry from the rock and roll career in her future. She was the first person to put a picture of a black bride in the *Plain Dealer*, but in 1989 admitted to *Scene*, "I thought she was Italian."[2]

A couple of years later, Scott graduated to writing a column on senior citizens called "Senior Class," and then in 1958 it began to fall into place when she took over the "Boy and Girl" column (later called "Teen Time"), in which she wrote about music that kids liked. September 15, 1964, was a fateful night for Jane. The Beatles played Cleveland for the first time, and she went to the show to review it. Already in her forties, Scott was considered too old to cover the rock beat. She didn't look the part of a rock and roller, either. She wore round, red glasses and tasteful skirts. When she attended rock shows, she'd bring earplugs, a PB&J sandwich in case she got hungry, safety pins, and toilet paper—she was prepared like a Girl Scout. After the Beatles performed, the mayor of Cleveland, Ralph J. Locher, banned more rock shows because he felt "rock concerts were like feeding narcotics to teenagers." That ban didn't last long. Two years later, in 1966, the Beatles returned to Cleveland and this time Scott interviewed them. "I realized I hit a chord," she told *SHOWcase* in 1989. "Rock is where they all were. I loved their show." Thus began forty years of her covering concerts and talking to esteemed musicians, everyone from Jim Morrison to (not so esteemed) Vanilla Ice.[3]

"Her history is fascinating," David Giffels tells me about Jane. "She had access that nobody could ever have imagined, in part because she was this loopy old lady who didn't look like she fit in with scene at all, but I think that was even more the reason why she endeared herself. And Bob Dylan loved her. Like Bob Dylan could love anybody. But anytime he would come to town, he would grant her access and greet her warmly."

In a 1979 *Rolling Stone* profile on Scott, she told them, "My age isn't a handicap. There's a certain advantage in being a mother figure." This "mother figure" encouraged Morrison to grant her an hour-long interview, in which he discussed religion. At this point she called herself the world's oldest teenager, which later led to the title "World's Oldest Rock Critic." Jane Scott became not only the first female music critic but also the first serious rock music critic of the vocation.[4]

"I knew Jane since I was about thirteen years old," David Spero tells me. "She came off as this little timid person who had such an amazing knowledge of rock and roll. She was just a wonderful, wonderful lady. If she didn't like somebody, she most likely wouldn't write about them as opposed to going out and trashing somebody. That wasn't her way. She also found a way to make Cleveland a part of her reviews. She'd talk to the kids in the audience and get their take on it."

It's true that Jane tried not to say or write anything negative about people—with the exception of Elvis Costello. He once got mad at her because after his show she asked him how it went. "He's scum.

But he sure can write," she told *Rolling Stone*. She helped launched Bowie's and Springsteen's careers, saying in 1975 that Springsteen was the next big thing. The movie *Almost Famous* is about a young rock critic named William who writes a story on a band. William's mentor, Lester Bangs, tells William he "cannot make friends with the rock stars." But he does anyway. The same thing happened with Scott. She wrote about these musicians and became close friends with some of them. Jane wrote about people in an informal way, which repeatedly won her awards, before and as she was working on her rock column. In 1974 she won first place at the Ohio Press Women's writing contest. In 1989 the city declared November 9 Jane Scott Day, and in 1991 she was inducted into the Cleveland Press Club Journalism Hall of Fame.

In 1987 national publications once again found renewed interest in Jane, who was almost seventy years old and still writing about rock music. *People* magazine, the *Wall Street Journal*, and *Star* magazine did features on her, probably fascinated with the novelty of an old lady who loved rock music so much. "It's always new and crazy and always changing," she told the *WSJ* about why she loved rock and roll.[5]

She combated ageism and misogyny in a male-dominated field of young people. "I don't like anything that puts down a woman, because we are one-half of the universe, and if it weren't for some, no man would be alive on earth. And I want them to remember that every now and then," she told the Associated Press.[6]

Annie Zaleski acknowledges what a trailblazer Scott was. "Growing up, she was a constant presence," she says. "She was familiar. She got the beat because no one else wanted it. But she treated all the bands with respect and she talked to them on their level and she didn't treat the music with condescension—she treated it from a genuine and dear place, and I think all musicians related to that. Everyone loved her from Springsteen to Bowie to the Beatles. Everyone knew Jane. And the fact that she was a woman—who kept doing it until her eighties—is inspirational. She was always herself."

In 2002, at the young age of eighty-three, Scott retired, after attending about ten thousand concerts and music events. She published her final column on April 12, 2002, a reminiscence about an Iggy Pop show. She wrote, "I didn't get splattered the night that punker Iggy Pop covered his chest and stomach with peanut butter and rolled around the Cleveland Agora stage like a dying trout." Her one regret was not starting her job earlier so she could've seen the first rock concert. "If I had begun on that Friday, March 21, 1952, I'd have gone to the first Moondog Coronation Ball at the old Arena, considered the world's first rock show," she wrote. "Think of the firsthand stories I'd still be writing about that night."[7]

Almost a decade after she hung up her earplugs, Scott died, on July 4, 2011, at ninety-two. A year later the Rock and Roll Hall of Fame installed a bronze memorial statue of her sitting on a bench, wearing her signature red glasses, inside the museum's lobby. She sits there smiling with a pencil and notepad, ready to engage with whomever sits next to her. That same year the Hall of Fame Library and Archives acquired her collection: twenty-four record cartons, thirty-one Hollinger boxes, fifteen oversize boxes, and fourteen audiovisual boxes containing photos, notepads, press clippings—you name it. In doing research for this book, I spent a day at the archives sifting through the Jane Scott Papers. In five hours I barely made a dent. She saved every ticket stub, press pass, photo, press clipping on herself and her writings, set lists, press kits on bands, postcards, and all of her indecipherable notepad scribbles. She was a pack rat, but the library organized it well. Without Jane Scott, Cleveland wouldn't have been quite the epicenter of the rock world. Rock criticism, which is a dying breed today, wouldn't have existed the way it did in the 1960s and beyond.

## SYSTEM 56

*System 23? No. System 49? Nah. System 84? Nope. System 56? Yes!*

—Steve Simenic

The most obscure—and one of the best—bands to hail from Cleveland is System 56. They played only five live shows and then broke up. While perusing Cleveland.com's list of "101 Most Important Songs in Cleveland-Akron Music History," I discovered the group. It took just one listen to their 1982 song "Metro-Metro" for me to be transcended—like when Dorothy arrives in Oz and her life goes from black-and-white to color.[8] Euro-Wave groups like Ultravox (the *Systems of Romance* album), Simple Minds, Gary Numan, and German group Kraftwerk influenced System 56's founder, Steve Simenic.

"I wanted to write a song about life in the city, about navigating some of those paradoxical emotional landscapes that lie somewhere between dislocation and exhilaration and how the changing cityscape affects the senses and the psyche—that sort of thing," Simenic says about the influence of "Metro-Metro." "Back then we were using an analog string machine run through a chorus effect box to 'thicken up' the sound of the strings, giving it that sort of trademark European lushness. Today nearly any garden-variety polyphonic keyboard has almost that same type of sound as one of its presets."

"Metro-Metro" is redolent of U2 guitars smashed against Simple Minds and Flock of Seagulls synth-rock. The melody is concurrently exuberant and filled with melancholy. Luckily, it got played on Cleveland's WMMS, so at least locals knew about the band. In October 1982 the group self-released (Detour Records) the six-song *Beyond the Parade* EP, which didn't include "Metro-Metro." "The original intention in putting the band together was to first record and release a record—in this case 'Metro-Metro' backed with 'In the Old World'—get some local college airplay, work up a set of ten to twelve songs, and play some gigs to support the single."

The foundation for System 56 harks back to the release of David
Bowie's then critically panned 1977 record *Low*, which was the first
in Bowie's Berlin Trilogy. "It was a definitive departure point for
much of the electronic synth-rock revolution to follow in the next
five years," Simenic says. "However, I wasn't quite ready to form
System 56 just yet. I needed some time to understand the recording
process and how to work with and construct my own sound using
a combination of guitars and synthesizers." In 1980 he released two
instrumental tracks under the name Aftermath. By 1981 Steve was
ready to form System 56. "It was going to be based on the Ultravox/
Simple Minds model—guitar, bass, synth, drums, and vocals." Steve
placed a want ad in the paper and found his lineup: Chuck Ryder on
bass, Kevin Lytle on synthesizers, Vince Scafiti on drums, and Steve
on guitar and lead vocals.

In 1982, in support of their singles, they played the Bank in Akron.
Then a couple of members departed the group. But once they settled
on a new lineup, they played three gigs in 1984, at Phantasy Theater
in Cleveland. There were actually two reasons for so few live shows,
but neither of them had anything to do with intentionally trying
to be reclusive or mysterious. "It just sort of seemed to work out
that way," Simenic says. They released the single "The Sounding," a
Simple Minds–inspired track. "The basic thrust behind 'The Sounding' was taking more of a thematic and even cinematic approach in
presenting a series of what you might call 'mini-vistas,' like slow,
wide-angle, panoramic shots in a movie. We were also starting to ex-
periment with more layered vocal arrangements, something which
our new bassist, Tom Lash, had suggested we try." Despite the band's
penchant for synths, Simenic doesn't think he stirred the synth-pop
inclinations of Reznor's Exotic Birds. "We knew the Exotic Birds and
would go see them play, but they were much more dance-oriented
than us," he says. "So I seriously doubt we were any influence on
them, or the industrial style of NIN or Filter."

So how did Simenic come up with the band's name? "Coming
from a technical background in electronics, I had always been in-

terested in various types of systems design, as well as cybernetics (the human-machine interrelationship)," he says. "The word 'system' seemed to have this subliminal appeal, and I suppose the title of *Systems of Romance* played some part as well. So when it came to naming the band, I started with that word and just added a number to it." He found that the number 56 sounded the best. "System 23? No. System 49? Nah. System 84? Nope. System 56? Yes! This is the type of geeky, alphanumeric minutiae only an OCD cyberneticist can truly appreciate."

The period the band was together, 1982–1984, was a thrilling time in music. Sounds from New Order, Depeche Mode, and others of that ilk were exported from overseas to the Midwest. The 2009 documentary *Synth Britannia* covers the topic of synth-based European groups from the 1970s and 1980s. "If there is one overarching takeaway that I would emphasize in all of this, it would be this: the original creative fire that drove much of this new genre was the result of the coming together of two different but highly complementary approaches—one in Britain, and the other in Germany," Simenic says. "The cross-pollination that occurred ignited an explosion of new music, which successfully merged the electronic sound and texture of the synthesizer with the archetypal rock template of guitar, bass, and drums, creating a synth-rock hybrid which subsequently evolved into all of its various permutations: New Wave, synth-pop, electronica, and EDM [electronic dance music]."

However, local punk bands also influenced Simenic. "In the late seventies, with punk mutating into post-punk, you'd be able to hear bands like Pere Ubu, Rocket from the Tombs, the Mice, the Pagans, and the early incarnation of Devo gigging in some of the smaller dives around town," he says. "I can remember going to see Devo at the Pirate's Cove in 1977, '78, where they would be screening their short film *The Truth About De-Evolution* while playing live on stage. No one knew quite what to make of them at the time, but that's how and where it all got started."

The amount of DIY and innovation that was happening overseas corresponds to what was happening in Northeast Ohio during those decades. "It's one of those well-kept secrets about Cleveland—the fan base there was very much aware of what was going on musically both in Britain and Europe, in a lot of different genres and styles of music, and had the vinyl to prove it," Simenic says. "At that time, Cleveland had a lot of rock and roll mojo in the air, resulting in a lot of contact going on not only between various musicians and bands but also between the radio DJs, the club owners, the record store people, and the music press. It was a very vibrant scene, and a lot of new bands were always coming through town, knowing they could get some exposure and sell a few records."

Unfortunately, System 56 didn't last long. "The breakup was a little bit of everything," he says. "I guess you could say some [of it was] related to personal friction within the band, some just a lack of cohesion and direction, and some related to creative exhaustion." After the band dissolved at the end of 1984, Simenic continued to work in music for a while. In 1990 he moved to Santa Barbara and eventually became an antiquarian book dealer. He wasn't too disappointed that the band ended the way it did, realizing it was inevitable. "Most record companies were already looking in other directions, and we would have likely appeared to be past our expiration date, to be perfectly honest. But no regrets."

In 2003 the band self-released *Retrospective: 1982–84*, a compilation of their singles, including "Metro-Metro"; *Beyond the Parade* songs; and three previously unreleased tracks, such as "The Sounding." In 2013 an Italian company called Synthetic Shadows reissued the record. Through the releases—and the internet—the band found more of a following in Europe and the United States. "Many of the younger fans were also discovering the band for the first time, so for them it wasn't nostalgia; it was fresh ground to be explored," Simenic says. "Each new generation connects to the music a bit differently, especially when it was likely made before they were even born. But what's more important is they still get it."

More than thirty years after "Metro-Metro" hit the airwaves, Simenic hopes System 56 will be remembered for "having the will and wherewithal to make some original music—and commit it to vinyl," he says. "That may sound like an oversimplification, but if we had channeled all of that energy into just playing those songs in a live setting, you and I would likely not be having this conversation today. There would have been little trace of System 56 remaining, other than a couple dozen more gigs that someone recalled seeing back in the day. When you have limited time and resources, you have to make the choice of what you want to be remembered for. Thus, here we are."

# 4

# COLUMBUS

THE MEGALOPOLIS OF COLUMBUS, NESTLED IN CENTRAL OHIO, is the one major city in Ohio whose population has not decreased since 1990. Even during the recession of 2008, the populous area sustained growth. Settled in 1812, Columbus is newer than both Cleveland (founded in 1796) and Cincinnati (settled in 1788). Its denizens haven't suffered the hardscrabble lives that other Ohio Rust Belt cities have. It's not littered with sputtered-out abandoned factories. Yet, according to Happy Chichester, singer-songwriter from Columbus rock bands Royal Crescent Mob and Howlin' Maggie, the city has soul.

"There is a spirit in Columbus that has been persistent since I've been active and observing," Chichester says, "and it's something I appreciate about the music scene, because there's diversity here, there's a rich community of musicians, there's an audience that encourages live music and original music and that's my favorite thing about Columbus—there's these deep roots. There's all these echoes of pop, rock, jazz, and funk." Chichester graduated from Northland High School, the alma mater of both country star Dwight Yoakam and Samuel Bayer, who directed Nirvana's "Smells Like Teen Spirit" music video. Dave Grohl and Joe Walsh briefly lived in town. In 1995 *Entertainment Weekly* wrote a three-page feature on the Columbus music scene, which didn't result in everyone in the local industry becoming rich and famous. Anyway Records owner Bela Koe-Krompecher thought the idea that they believed Columbus was the next Seattle was "absurd."[1]

"Columbus has a lot of punk bands that result from people like Eric Davidson coming down from Cleveland to go to OSU [Ohio State University] making a band here, and we get the New Bomb Turks," Chichester says. "For a long time I thought to get your foot in the door with an audience in the early nineties you had to have some punk aspect. There had to be some kind of kicking-down-the-doors sort of vibe to your music."

"In town, a lot of the bands weren't exactly a punk band or a hardcore band, or weren't exactly a grunge band," Davidson says. "People in Ohio appreciate when bands are a little weirder and don't fall into an exact genre. Even the Raspberries, when they had top-forty hits—their songs were sad and always about not being big enough. They never got the girl, and they never had a number one hit. Columbus is a more rural town. It's more laid back than Cleveland, but it's not quite as sarcastic as Cleveland. We didn't fit in there, either places." (The area's bucolic aspect led to Columbus being nicknamed "Cowtown" and to Tony Barnett starting an entertainment newspaper called *Moo*.) While on tour, when people discovered that Davidson was from Ohio, they'd ask him, "'What's in the water up there?' I hear that about Ohio more than anywhere else. I do think there's a strain of weird, dark, sort of funny music that comes out of Ohio. It usually means no sales, though."

"New Bomb Turks, Thomas Jefferson Slave Apartments—they are the ones that laid the path for the bands that I play in," says Philip Kim, who moved from the Cleveland area to attend OSU and plays bass in the local group Connections. The band has released several albums on Columbus label Anyway Records. They came together in 2012, with Kevin Elliott, brother of Adam Elliott from Times New

Viking (the three-piece and once nationally touring "shitgazers"). Members of the group have day jobs and family lives that prevent them from hitting the road a lot. "We live comfortably enough to make music," Kim says. "We do have a lot of people who stay, so you have a network of older musicians and veteran bands who hang out and go to the bars that other kids go to. We all hang out together, and that helps in having people to talk to about how their experiences have been." One of those hangouts is music venue/bar Ace of Cups (since 2011), on High Street, near campus. "It's like church—everyone knows each other there," but back in the day Stache's (its building was torn down in 1997), Little Brother's, and Bernies Bagels and Deli were the go-to venues for shows.[2]

Chichester sees the camaraderie, too, and says the turf is bereft of competition among bands. "That's another thing I like about Columbus—I don't hear or experience or feel any backstabbing professional jealousy. The musicians themselves, as far as I can see—and I've been at it awhile—seem supportive and enthusiastic. I don't hear any scuttlebutt of people being jealous."

Though the students from OSU are what keeps downtown and Short North purring, Kim notices a "lack connecting with the university, which is obviously a huge demo of young kids who love music," he says. "You don't see too many of those kids coming to shows. There are many theories to why that is. That's a weird thing with Columbus in terms of the music scene."

In the mid-2000s, Times New Viking and Psychedelic Horseshit represented Cowtown's indie scene well but then dispersed into other bands. "If there's a new band in town that's decent, every publication will write an article about them," Kim says. "People will post their music and you'll see a big spike in activity, and then a few months later you don't hear much about them anymore. The attention span of people is so short, there's short bursts of interest and people are looking for the next band. For us, we go slow and steady. I guess we're kind of like a band's band or a critic's band."

But in 2017 Ohio's capital city experienced a supernova in local duo Twenty One Pilots, who won a Grammy (out of five nominations) for Best Pop Duo/Group Performance and accepted the award pantless. In the moment, Tyler Joseph and Josh Dun gave a shout-out to their neck of the woods. "This story, it starts in Columbus, Ohio," Joseph said. (They grew up there and didn't move there for the university.) A thrum had been building for the group since 2009, when they self-released their first album. In 2011, not yet signed to Warner-owned record label Fueled by Ramen, Twenty One Pilots sold out the seventeen-hundred-seat Newport Pavilion in Columbus. They eventually signed and released two records, including the award-winning (and platinum-selling) *Blurryface*. (The record landed in the top ten best-selling records of 2016, next to *Adele*.)

The band combines elements of rock, rap, and punk, and performs head-scratching Elvis covers live. "My friend listened to them and said, 'It's like if you took your music on your iPod and hit shuffle—every song is different than the one before,'" Davidson says. "Maybe that's why they're popular." As a thank-you for Columbus's support, in 2017 Twenty One Pilots played a series of intimate club shows around town. Unlike fellow duo the Black Keys, they didn't seem to struggle for years before winning a Grammy. Maybe that's the difference between ascending in a pre-internet versus post-internet world. "Most of us in the scene don't like their music and kind of roll our eyes," Kim says. "They are on a different end of the spectrum than most bands here."

### ANYWAY RECORDS

*There's no money in putting records out. . . . People don't buy records.*

—Bela Koe-Krompecher

Bela Koe-Krompecher, a fixture of the Columbus music scene, has spent most of his life in Ohio. As an adolescent he lived in Athens and Springfield (an oppressive small town, he says), and moved to Columbus after high school, in the late eighties. In 1992 he and

Gaunt guitarist and lead singer Jerry Wick founded Anyway Records in the basement of Used Kids Records, where they worked as
clerks. Since then, he's put out more than eighty records of mostly
Ohio-based groups, such as a Gaunt seven-inch single, "Jim Mother-
fucker"; a New Bomb Turks live EP; Athens bluegrass-rock group
Appalachian Death Ride's debut LP; Thomas Jefferson Slave Apartments' *Straight to Video*; an Ass Ponys full-length; and a few seven-
inch Guided by Voices singles.

"There's no money in putting records out," he says. "People don't
buy records. They stream music. Record stores used to be the center
of activity—that's where everybody gathered, and Used Kids was
that." Anyway hasn't netted much of a profit, not even in the nineties,
but producing CDs is cheaper now than it was decades ago; vinyl is
still expensive to manufacture. Vinyl sales started increasing in the
2010s, but so has streaming. "I think for a label like mine, my goal is
to break even, but I think kids buy records just to have the record,"
he says. "I don't think that's how they're listening to it. When I look
at my royalty statements, by far the most listens are digital. A band
like Connections has hundreds of thousands of streams. But there
literally is no money, because you're looking at one-thirtieth of a
cent per Spotify stream. I'll go in to Used Kids and it's mostly re-
issues. I don't know if someone discovering new music would go to a
record store today." Pre-streaming, music fans would find out about
new music through college radio or visiting a place like Used Kids.
People's attention spans are shorter now in that they don't spend as
much time inhaling music as they did decades ago.

Despite bands that have released records in Ohio, the state has
not channeled much of a "music industry machinery," instead creating micro labels in Anyway, OKra, Columbus Discount Records,
and Scat (no longer based in Ohio). Major indie labels Matador, Sub
Pop, and IRS didn't exist here, and Bela Koe-Krompecher thinks
it's because inland labels don't have the same access to money as
those on the coasts do. "When I started Anyway, I never had any
money," he says. "Robert Griffin [of the band Prisonshake] ran Scat

Records out of Cleveland and never had any money, even though he put out *Bee Thousand.*" In order to distribute it, he signed a deal with Matador. "It was a weird spot—even if you had a hit, like he did with Guided by Voices, he couldn't keep it in print, because the money wasn't coming in from the indie distributors like Matador," he says. "I think that's one reason why a lot of the bands that might've been bigger at one time never got as big publicly as they should have. A lot of kids who go to school in Boston or New York had money, so they could tour. People from Ohio don't come from money."

Koe-Krompecher mentions singer/songwriter Jenny Mae, who received positive reviews in mainstream publications, yet she didn't break out of Columbus or anywhere else. "There's no reason why she couldn't have been as big as Veruca Salt or someone like that," he says. Sadly, Mae passed away in August 2017. "Appalachian Death Ride was great. In Seattle they would've been part of that whole scene, but where they're from, Athens, they just can't." Even Guided by Voices were underappreciated. Koe-Krompecher and Ron House of Thomas Jefferson Slave Apartments helped Bob Pollard get in touch with Scat, which connected with Matador to get his records released. "You listen to some of those Guided by Voices records and think, 'Why didn't they become as big as Arcade Fire?' That's a bit of Dayton's 'fuck you, we're just going to do it our way.'"[3]

In 1995 Anyway signed with distributor Revolver to absorb some of the cost of pressing the records and to cast a wider net with getting the releases into larger markets. "I would come up with the record and they'd manufacture and distribute it," Koe-Krompecher says. Torn between offers from Revolver and Caroline Records, he chose the former. "Caroline was owned by Virgin at the time, and they were signing up every little label like mine, and I thought it'd get lost." There are more bands putting out records today than ever, yet it's harder to manage a label. The window for acquiring hype for your record, according to Koe-Krompecher, lasts only a month now, as opposed to the seventies through the nineties, when releases had legs. "You have a month to sell a record, and then it's old," he says.

"People don't want to write about it." Although the window is tiny, the digital industry has generated more platforms for bands to get heard and read about: NPR has done pieces on Anyway artists Connections and St. Lenox.

While running Anyway in the nineties, Koe-Krompecher booked shows and would go out as many as five times a week, so he became a figurehead on the scene. He liked to pair up local bands with nationally touring bands, the scene bolstered by the amity between regional bands. "A band would play OU [Ohio University], and then the bands they played with would come up to Columbus," he says. "Scrawl did shows with Afghan Whigs [Marcy Mays of the trio Scrawl sang lead vocals on their song "My Curse"], so you'd have that as well. They'd do shows because they didn't have anything else to do. Back then you had two bars you could go to see bands—it was either Bernies or Stache's." However, in the mid-eighties the drinking age in Ohio increased from nineteen to twenty-one, curtailing a lot of youngsters from going to shows at bars.

In some ways Koe-Krompecher thinks Columbus's music scene was better in the 2010s than twenty years prior, and that has to do with the way major labels gobbled up and spat out local bands. Elektra dropped Scrawl, which had previously run into issues with Rough Trade. Warner Bros. dismissed Gaunt, and Jim Shepard's band V-3 signed to American Recordings (owned by mega-producer Rick Rubin) subsidiary Onion, but then got cut. "Jim put out esoteric stuff and some of it was brilliant, but he signed to a major label. What were they thinking?," Koe-Krompecher says.

"Growing up in the eighties, you could discover there was this whole underground scene," he says.

> While that was going on, you had this foundation being built of record stores, clubs, and bands doing the circuit in playing the Euclid Tavern [in Cleveland], Bernies, and the Union [in Athens]. You had that going on in the eighties and early nineties, so you had a micro music industry that was so far off the radar of the major labels. But when Sonic Youth signed to Geffen Records with 1990's *Goo*, it gave permission for everybody to sign bands, because we were always like 'fuck you' to the major labels because they were

the enemy. They were the ones who were putting out Whitney Houston and Huey Lewis and the News. There wasn't danger to any mainstream music in the eighties. So if you wanted that, you went underground.

Nirvana's thirty-million-selling record *Nevermind* turned the industry inside out in the fall of 1991. "The music industry said we're going to find as many things as we can like that and throw it against the wall and see who survives," Koe-Krompecher says. "Ohio was good because we had all of these bands already." V-3, Thomas Jefferson Slave Apartments, Gaunt, and Scrawl signed their lives away and got burned. "The major labels didn't understand how the circuit worked," he says. "It was sad, because you saw bands getting signed, putting one record out, and the band getting dropped."

In 1997 Dayton had its tragedy with Brainiac, and almost four years later Capital City had its own tragedy when Jerry Wick of Gaunt died. On the morning of January 10, 2001, Wick was riding home on his bicycle, carrying a pizza, when a car hit and killed him. He was only thirty-three. This occurred soon after Warner Bros. dropped his band (as a result, the band broke up), and it came on the heels of three other local deaths, including Jim Shepard's suicide in 1998. The deaths sent ripples through the close-knit music community, and it shook Koe-Krompecher into sobriety. "Jerry was my best friend for years," he says.

> We hung out the day he died. He was struggling with his alcoholism and his depression. Jerry wanted to be famous. Now Jerry would be thrilled by the way people talk about him. Gaunt was never very popular here. When you're young, you tend to put your eggs all in one basket, at least emotionally, which isn't the smartest thing. I wouldn't say I was bitter or even disillusioned; I was just minorly crushed by all of these things that had happened. So I took a break and got sober and went back to school. You saw a lot of other bands, people like me, making life changes. That was the death knell of being young.

Many of Koe-Krompecher's friends either left town or settled down and quit music. Wick's passing represented a harbinger for the winnowing of the music industry as everyone had known it. "Those of us in the record store industry, our sales started slipping," he says.

"You knew something was coming but you didn't know what it was. We weren't making as much money."

The Columbus indie band Connections has released a few albums with Anyway. I asked bassist Philip Kim what Bela taught him about being in a signed band. "Managing expectations—I think that's a big one—and not to get too excited in general, and be grateful for whatever we can get," Kim says. "Any little show in town is committing to having a good time and playing the best you can, and not being too disappointed if not many people come, because that's always going to happen. Managing disappointment and expectations makes it easier to have a good time and not worry about too much except playing well."

The industry Koe-Krompecher cultivated in the nineties may be worlds apart now, but he thinks there are still throngs of good contemporary musicians in Ohio. Anyway limits itself to three to five releases a year, mainly because Koe-Krompecher's family and his job as a social worker eat up most of his time. And, of course, there's no money in it. But, he says, he has stuck with it for so long because he loves music and "because no one else was going to put those records out."

### HOWLIN' MAGGIE // ROYAL CRESCENT MOB

*It can't be done, so we might as well do it.*

—Happy Chichester

Happy Chichester began his music career as a teen playing in Ray Fuller and the Bluesrockers and then joined the funk four-piece Royal Crescent Mob, a Columbus band that formed in the mid-eighties and set the template for other local groups to follow. "I started professionally playing bass and being able to pay the rent with my music with Ray Fuller and the Bluesrockers," Chichester says. "We were playing all over the place. I was a teenager and traveling around Pennsylvania, Indiana, Kentucky, Michigan. I was an

awestruck young guy. Royal started recording its first record and I
didn't want to go back to school." He took the plunge and dropped
out of Ohio University (similar to Brainiac's John Schmersal) to do
music full-time. "There was no insurance it was going to do anything
for us," he says. "As it turned out, the *Village Voice* named *Land of
Sugar* the EP of the year and we got Carlton [Smith, drummer] and
it took off like a rocket. That band was the most awe-inspired, won-
drous thing for a young person like myself to have experienced. It
gave me almost a college education in itself."

Though R. C. Mob formed in Columbus, its underpinnings de-
rived from a time Chichester and the Ray Fuller Band played a gig
in Athens and stayed at Marcy Mays's house afterward. "She let us
crash at her house and the three of us that later formed Royal Crescent Mob were standing around her record player and listening to
side six of Marvin Gaye's anthology. When 'Inner City Blues' came
on we looked at each other, and that moment I think we thought,
'We're going to maybe do something outside of this current band
we're in and do something more rhythmic and gritty'—not that
Ray's not gritty—but I think we wanted to play more funk stuff."
Chichester found more inspiration in the region. "It's an attitude of
'Well, it can't be done, so we might as well do it,'" he says.

> So you get these innovations that are combining things that haven't been
> combined before—Devo coming out of Kent after the shootings. NIN
> created something new. The Ohio Players were a self-contained band. They
> weren't under the control of a big label or producer. They did their thing from
> within the band itself. Rahsaan Roland Kirk [an influential jazz musician
> born in Columbus]—nobody ever sounded like that before or since. Royal
> Crescent Mob has a bass drum in the Ohio exhibit at the Hall of Fame
> museum, and it's right between Roger Troutman's bass [from the band Zapp]
> and Tommy James's electric guitar. To me that's a pretty good example of an
> Ohio sound. Funk and pop—it's so diverse.

The group released two records on Sire and then called it quits
after their seventh and final record, *Good Lucky Killer*, in 1994. Soon
after, Chichester cobbled together another quartet, Howlin' Maggie,
an alt-rock group that reeked of the music being generated in the

mid-nineties. "I named the band after my grandmother," he says. "I was named after her husband, my grandfather. When I was in college, my mother told me a story of my grandmother shooting my grandfather and he survived. She shot him twice, apparently, and not only he survived but their marriage survived. I thought it was extraordinary. I wrote that story down and jotted the title and called it Howlin' Maggie."

Chichester performed most of the band's instrumental and vocal duties—alongside future NIN drummer Jerome Dillon—and their first of only two records, *Honeysuckle Strange*, came out on Columbia Records in 1996. The songs "Alcohol" and "I'm a Slut" had edge to them but were also infectious, pop-based music. "My band, I made sure they had a steady salary and health insurance, but that's almost completely unheard of nowadays," Chichester says. "It was a real music scene back then. There was money flowing in and economics going for it, which is not the case nowadays. Bands are pretty much on their own and there's not a lot of outside support. The nineties, though, was a pretty good time to be rockin', because I feel like that attitude that I described about Ohio—it can't be done, so we might as well do it—was on full display." He played shows with other local bands like Guided by Voices and Brainiac. "There's so much music in all those bands, just such outlandish sound and style and writing. It's a richness. I feel very proud to have been a part of it."

In 2001, now with a new lineup—including Carlton Smith from R. C. Mob—Howlin' Maggie released *Hyde* on Chichester's own label, PopFly. (In 2016 the band reunited and did some shows where they played the record in its entirety.) After Howlin' Maggie concluded, Chichester played on a couple of Afghan Whigs records and an album of Greg Dulli's offshoot band, Twilight Singers. Chichester lost interest in Twilight Singers and in 2002 started releasing solo records on his label. He still lives in Columbus and ponders how Ohio State has always acted as a conduit for the music scene. "For the longest time the bars around campus were this hub of a music scene," he says. "The kids from the suburbs would come in and go to those venues on High Street across from OSU. Having a good college provides an audience and helps to give some strength to the scene. Some people come to college here and end up staying here and making music." But he says the music venues are more spread out now. "The music is less centered around OSU. You can find original music in suburbs much more now than you used to. The sound diversified, which seemed to open up the musical sound more. Ohio produces really good and innovative music year in and year out. It's astonishing," he says. "We don't have an ocean. There are no mountains to climb. There's not much snowboarding. It's like, well, we're going to get in the garage or basement and rock our heads off."

### NEW BOMB TURKS

*If somebody came along and seemed cool, believe me, we would've taken a*
*million-dollar deal.... We would've taken a hundred-thousand [dollar] deal.*

—Eric Davidson

Punkster Eric Davidson moved from Cleveland to Columbus in 1987 to attend OSU. He brought the din of Cleveland with him and pulverized it into his garage-punk band New Bomb Turks. Through the group he would spend the next twelve years forging Cowtown's burgeoning indie-rock scene. "Growing up in Cleveland, I didn't think of Ohio as conservative at all," Davidson says. "It was union heavy. It was a weird mix of people and foods and languages, and it was an old city. And then when I went to Columbus, it was a slap in the face: *Oh, I see.* It dawned on me there are a lot of parts of Ohio that are very conservative." He didn't let that deter him from organizing a rather strident punk band with students Jim Weber, Bill Randt, and Matt Reber. Though Davidson liked to sing and the other guys played in bands in high school, this was their first professional band. Davidson met Jim in the dorms, and the two had a radio show on campus, which is where they met Reber, who knew Randt. All of them hailed from the Cleveland area.

"Jim and I liked the established local bands—Scrawl, Great Plains—but we weren't seeing any brand-new bands around town that we were much into, not the kind of punk stuff we were listening to," Davidson says. "We probably said to each other we could try to get our band going, and if we play, maybe we can bring in out-of-town bands and maybe we'll find kindred spirits that way—and that's exactly what happened." In 1990 New Bomb Turks played their first gig, at local watering hole Stache's. At first the group didn't think far ahead. "I remember thinking the early bands that we were compared to in reviews were the Lazy Cowgirls, the Dead Boys, and the Devil Dogs, all these bands that never sold a million records," he says, "but bands that I really loved. They never sold a million records, so why would I expect suddenly we would?"

Crypt Records, run by Tim Warren, an American living in Hamburg, Germany, asked them to record an album; *!!Destroy-Oh-Boy!!* was released in 1993. "That got me thinking, okay, we have to decide how long do we want to do this and how serious do we want to take it," he says. "The independent music world was growing a lot more at that time." The Turks dodged the major label craze (and hiring a manager), unlike their brethren Scrawl (Elektra) and Gaunt (Warner Bros.). In retrospect Davidson thinks that if they had signed to Warner Bros. or someone like that, they "would've had to change their sound dramatically." After releasing a few more albums for Crypt, they signed to major indie Epitaph. "If somebody came along and seemed cool, believe me, we would've taken a million-dollar deal," he says. "We would've taken a hundred-thousand [dollar] deal. Epitaph came along and it was decent money, they had great distribution throughout the whole world, and they had some bands at the time I liked. So we went with that." In 1996 Epitaph released *Scared Straight*, the band's third full-length.

"There was so much money in the music industry at the time to fly record label guys in, take bands out to dinner, and buy a few rounds in bars," he says. "It was a vacation for them. They didn't have any real interest in signing bands unless someone really blew them away. It was a chance to get out of New York, Chicago, and Los Angeles for the weekend and have someone fly you to fucking Columbus to get loaded with a bunch of college kids."

New Bomb Turks did make a point to tour outside of Ohio, which is something Davidson thinks more local bands should've done. "There were a lot of great bands in the area during the eighties, and no one has heard of any of them, because they never got out of town. They never committed to being a real band: quit your job for a little while, tour for a few weeks, do something. Get out there. Put a record out. Try to at least play regionally. Most of these bands never got out of Cleveland. It's that attitude of 'Fuck it, no one is going to care anyway.'" Davidson thinks one reason why bands weren't able to leave Ohio and tour had to do with lack of funds, something Bela Koe-Krompecher discussed, too. "I didn't know hardly any rich kids in Cleveland, because they didn't have Dad's platinum card to buy a tour van and tour. Cleveland bands end up stewing in their cold basements over the winter and come up with weird sounds."

Royal Crescent Mob, Great Plains, and Scrawl came up the ranks in the mid-eighties and gave Columbus's music scene its pulse. "There wasn't a long history of a DIY scene to lean back on," Davidson says. "Columbus didn't have a scene going back to the seventies, so everyone was learning it on the fly. Bernies had jam bands or nothing at all." Davidson felt Columbus used to exemplify a college town and a destination for the Ohio State Fair—that's it. "It was organic forming this indie-rock thing in the nineties," he says. "It's continued. Now Columbus does have a set indie underground tradition that goes back to the mid-eighties, but it didn't when I got there. Everything was pretty new."

The reason bands thrived in the nineties, Davidson muses, was because after the musicians graduated, the contingent stayed in town instead of moving elsewhere, such as Marcy Mays, who turned her focus to Ace of Cups after her band Scrawl deactivated in the late nineties. In 1999 Randt departed New Bomb Turks, and Sam Brown took his place as drummer. (Brown played in Spoon/Wolf Parade supergroup Divine Fits, who in 2012 played one of their first shows as a band at Ace of Cups, with Connections.) After putting out their tenth full-length, the rollicking *Switchblade Tongues & Butterknife Brains*, in 2003, New Bomb Turks technically broke up, but they're still friends and play shows. In 2004, after almost two decades eking out a living in Columbus, Davidson took off for the more expensive New York. "Columbus is a really easy town to throw the couch on the front porch of a house and stay there getting high for the next ten years," he says. "It's nice in a lot of ways, but I was getting tired of it." In 2010 he wrote a book about punk rockers, *We Never Learn: The Gunk Punk Undergut, 1988–2001*, featuring interviews with many Ohio and international punk bands.[4]

New Bomb Turks made a big dent on the punk scene, both in Columbus and in globe-trotting the world. But could they have been bigger? "Yeah, maybe we could've reached a bigger audience," Davidson says.

> I'm proud of our band. I like our records, but I'm not going to sit here and be like, we should've been bigger. The things we would've had to do [on a major label] would've led to a lot of infighting, and there were so many one-hit wonders in the era and so many bands that got signed and were the butt of a joke a year later. We didn't want to be one of those. We all got through this without any of us dying of an overdose. We toured the world sixty times. I had never been on a commercial jet until I went to Europe with the band. I was broke growing up. That's pretty good. If somebody would've told me that when I started the band I'd be able to do all the stuff we did and still remain friends with people, I would've considered that success.

The triumph of bands like New Bomb Turks inspired more indie bands to form in Columbus, such as Times New Viking, who were on Matador and Merge. "Because of Times New Viking and bands in their orbit in the 2000s, indie-rock has a real history now, just like Chapel Hill, North Carolina," Davidson says. "I think Columbus has just as much if not more of a history of coming up with bands in the past twenty-five years than most similarly sized towns in the country. There was never a big hit out of it. There was never a

Nirvana-like hit band that came out of the scene, but I think Columbus is really respected to the country on the indie-rock level."

## SINKANE

*Kids from Ohio grow up with a more open mind or
realistic mind of what the world is like.*

—Ahmed Gallab (Sinkane)

"I was born in London—my father was a diplomat. He was working for the city's embassy," Ahmed Gallab, aka Sinkane, says. "We moved from London to Sudan. In 1989 the government that my father was affiliated with was overthrown. We came to the United States around the same time it got overthrown. My father was essentially exiled from the country, so we applied for asylum in United States. We had to figure something out. From there, my father and mother went back to school and we lived in Utah for a while, and I moved to Ohio in 1996."

Gallab was not born in the United States, yet he lived in Kent, Ohio, during his adolescent years. The music of Kent—and later Columbus—influenced him as an artist. Since 2007 Gallab has played under the moniker Sinkane, a name that comes from a misheard Kanye West lyric. In the Jay-Z/West song "Never Let Me Down," they rap about a slave named Cinque, who in the 1800s was involved in a slave revolt on the *Amistad* ship. "I'm an African person; how do I not know about Sinkane?" Gallab says. Turns out, he heard the name wrong. "There must be some guy named Sinkane. This is too good of a name. There wasn't. It was time for me to put out my first record and I needed a name and it was Google-proof and it sounded cool, and I'm like, maybe I'll become Sinkane."

Years before Gallab transmogrified into an electronic-afro-funk star, he had to learn the ropes in a sometimes homogenous culture. "I think more of the culture shock was the distances between the places I lived in the United States, not the distance between the United States and Sudan," he says. While living in Provo, Utah, he was one of the only people who wasn't Mormon, and he was the only black kid in his school. "When you're living amongst people who believe in the same thing as you and they do the same things as you do, when something different comes along it's weird and doesn't make any sense," he says. At the age of eleven he and his family settled down in Kent (his father taught at Hiram College in nearby Hiram, Ohio), and suddenly Gallab found diversity.

> In Ohio, everyone in my high school had different beliefs, and they came from different backgrounds. They understood things differently. There wasn't a single Mormon in my school. There were many different people that came from different ideologies and some people who didn't believe in religion. That's very big as a young kid to experience that kind of energy. Also, my middle school and my high school were almost 60 percent black. Kids from Ohio grow up with a more open mind or realistic mind of what the world is like. With that said, there's a lot of things people in Ohio don't experience growing up as well. For me, it was nice to get thrown into a community that was so diverse in Kent.

In Kent Gallab felt connected to the hard-core and punk scenes, because they catered to outsiders. "They found solace in DIY," he says. "The music was profound because it was super intense and super immediate, and it felt like everyone in the hard-core scene was using hard-core as a catharsis. They needed to purge out their anger or their resentment or their angst as fast as they could, so the music was fast and super loud and it made me feel really good. It put me in a safe place." At the age of fourteen Gallab started playing drums. He listened to bands from the Kent-based record label Donut Friends—the Party of Helicopters, Harriet the Spy, and the Man I Fell in Love With. He liked Churchbuilder, a synth-pop group from the Black Keys' Pat Carney. "Those were the bands that shaped my understanding [of music]," he says. "This was my life from age fourteen until I got out of college. I probably went to almost every indie-rock show in Cleveland between 2000 and 2004. I was always at shows. It was my favorite thing to do." In 2002 Gallab moved to Columbus to attend Ohio State, where he submerged himself in the local atmosphere. He attended and booked shows at the Legion of

Doom punk house, near campus, and loved the band Times New Viking. "They came up around the same time as we did. We'd always play shows together and hang out."

Gallab moved from to Columbus to Brooklyn shortly after graduating. He played drums, guitar, and bass as a session member for indie bands Caribou, Of Montreal, and Yeasayer before venturing on his own. In 2007 he dropped *Sinisterlas*, followed by *Color Voice*. In 2012 he released the full-length *Mars* on DFA, the New York–based label cofounded by LCD Soundsystem front man James Murphy. In 2014 City Slang released the full-length *Mean Love*, and in 2017 they released *Life & Livin' It*; the album cover features a shopping bag from the Columbus record store Used Kids. "I bought so many records from that place," he says. "It's one of the best records stores I've ever been to in my life." He intentionally made the new record "joyful" because of the current political climate. "We're living in a tough time and it sucks, but you have to accept the fact this is what reality is, and you have to move on and do something about it. You have to have a solution, and my solution is to stay positive and to create as much positive energy as possible and to inspire people to make change with that positivity."

Sinkane unleashed the good vibes in his Brooklyn borough, his home since 2008. So how does the New York music scene differ from Ohio? "I think the biggest difference is people come to Brooklyn hoping their band is going to make it or strike big, or their idea of music is they could be famous," he says. "You rarely hear someone say, 'I'm moving to Columbus for music.' They might say that, but they're not saying it in the same way they would if they were saying they're moving to Brooklyn for music. I think the music scene is more comfortable in Ohio. I think people in New York take music more seriously in a way that they don't in Ohio. They're more political." He further elaborates on the distinction between Ohio groups and those in bigger cities.

One of the reasons why there are so many great bands from Ohio is because you don't live in LA or New York or Chicago. You don't have this open access to the things you do in New York and Chicago. You gain a sense of creativity that doesn't exist in any big town. People from Ohio are dreamers and they're idealistic and they romanticize things and they create these stories in their head of what they perceive music to be, which is different from people from New York. A lot of people in Ohio have soul. They might not be the best musicians, but they're very soulful. Even [metal band] Mushroomhead from Cleveland—they're all soulful. That creates a different kind of song and I think people relate to that.

Gallab thinks it's strange to want to be in a band, something his parents didn't comprehend at first. "You're doing it because you want to have fun and don't give a shit," he says. "My parents didn't understand that for a long time: 'Why would you go on tour and only give yourself five dollars a day to eat food? That doesn't make any sense.' It's a weird experience, but what you gain is something that you'll never forget for the rest of your life. It was a catharsis for me." Sometimes while on tour he runs into his old Columbus friends in random places. "It's really weird when you see someone in Paris who you used to get drunk with when you were twenty-two at a local shitty bar like Bernies." Even though Sinkane left Columbus years ago, his experiences left a remarkable impression on him. "Columbus was a very important part of my life," he says. "If it wasn't for living there and meeting the people and befriending them, then I wouldn't be the person that I am today. I'm very much indebted to that city and the punk scene there and the punk community and everybody who helped me become who I am."

### NELSONVILLE MUSIC FESTIVAL

*Ohio is a melting pot of the melting pot.... It's not a very dualistic*
*place. It's a swing state. It's a purple state. You can experience a lot of*
*different cultures in Ohio, and it creates a well-rounded thing.*

— Leo DeLuca

Ohio puts on various music festivals every year, but none can compete with Appalachia's Nelsonville Music Festival (NMF), an hour southeast of Columbus, which Tim Peacock founded in 2005 as a fund-raiser for Stuart's Opera House, an 1800s historic performing arts venue located in the town's Public Square. The fest began as a one-day event but in 2012 morphed into a four-day festival of bluegrass, folk, singer/songwriter, and rock acts playing at Robbins Crossing, on the grounds of Hocking College in Nelsonville, Ohio. Over the years, countrified mainstays like Willie Nelson, Loretta Lynn, and the Avett Brothers have performed at the fest, along with the Flaming Lips, Randy Newman, Guided by Voices, and Wilco. The daily attendance has swelled to about seventy-five hundred people, compared to less than one thousand in the beginning. Diversity ranks front and center here, with several women-fronted acts playing during the idyllic weekend.

Brian Koscho, who has been marketing manager for both the festival and the opera house since 2007, says they've eschewed the typical sponsorship route that a lot of bigger fests take. "It's just a different model," he says. "For Nelsonville Music Fest, our investors are our sponsors and donors." That means attendees will not see stages named after Bud Light, or for that matter, many corporate vendors. It should be noted that at the 2017 NMF, all of the beer—and I mean all of it—was sourced from independent local and regional breweries, including four based in nearby Athens, Ohio.

I've been to a lot of music festivals all over the country, but Southeast Ohio's NMF is mellower than the others. It could be the folksy aspect of a free music stage, called Boxcar, situated next to an old boxcar and nonfunctioning train tracks. Another stage is the No-Fi Cabin, a twenty-five-seat schoolhouse with no electricity, which peddles harmonica-laced acoustic performances. Kids twelve and under get free admission, and the Kids Zone area entertains them with people dressed up in arty puppet costumes and a variety of activities. The best part about the fest is its zero waste policy: they try to compost and recycle everything. Plastic cups are not provided, so in order to drink beer or drinking fountain water, you pay a small fee and then are provided with a reusable cup that you can take home with you.

The 2017 fest took place during the first weekend in June. I visited Sarah Jessica Parker's hometown for one day (the second day of the fest) to watch Ohio acts like Leggy (a punkish guy-girl trio from Cincinnati), St. Lenox (a one-man band from Columbus who is signed to Anyway Records), and Cloud Nothings (Cleveland rockers) set Athens County ablaze. Cloud Nothings performed their mutinous songs in the early evening and jolted everyone from their post-afternoon haze. The lawn-chair jockeys sat farther back in the field than the front's fist-pumping throngs, but the smiles on their faces clearly expressed their feeling that Cloud Nothings have killed it. A couple of hours later, the night's headliners, They Might Be Giants, attracted legions of people to hear their comical tunes.

While charging my phone at the solar charging station (of course they have solar panels), I ran into Leo DeLuca, a musician/music journalist from the Dayton suburb of Oakwood, and percussionist of the Athens-Dayton folk-rock group Southeast Engine, who have played the fest a few times. DeLuca's bandmate Adam Remnant performed a solo show earlier to a rapt crowd inside the No-Fi Cabin. Most recently, DeLuca played drums for R. Ring, and Southeast Engine may or may not be on hiatus. "It's more nebulous than that," DeLuca says.

After graduating from Oakwood High School, DeLuca and Remnant attended Ohio University in Athens and started the band— Jesse Remnant and Billy Matheny joined several years later—in 1999. "Southeast Engine is an amalgamation of Dayton underground and Athens folk scene," DeLuca says. They found a permanent legacy in Athens when local pizzeria Avalanche Pizza named a vegetarian pie after them. While growing up in Dayton in the nineties, De-Luca remembers when Guided by Voices, the Breeders, and Brainiac broke out on a national level. Akin to Griffin and Nathan Hamill (see Dayton chapter), DeLuca has a lifelong obsession with Brainiac. At fourteen he saw them play a local show. "I had to stand on a chair to see them play, because I couldn't see," he says. "The environment scared the living shit out of me. I was intimidated as hell, but it was still the greatest show of my life. It opened this whole new world for me." DeLuca thinks that when Brainiac's Tim Taylor died in 1997, it "took the air out of Dayton's tires" and concluded the focus on the city's music scene. "Death has that effect on things," says Bela Koe-Krompecher, who is also with us and charging his phone. (Fun fact: Most everyone in Ohio's music world knows one another.)

We talk about how twenty years ago, making a record was more difficult than today because, as DeLuca puts it, "you had to roll up your sleeves and take your craft seriously." Studio time cost a lot more money back then, but it didn't always result in a record that sounded good. "You can come to something like this that has so much new music and there's thousands and thousands of people here wanting to experience it," Koe-Krompecher says. "In a way, it's re-freshing—people are still finding new music somehow. A band like Cloud Nothings can have four thousand people watching them and being into it. I don't think that could have happened in the nineties."

Misra Records, a former Dayton-based label, released multiple Southeast Engine titles; DeLuca managed the label from 2010 to 2015. However, it turned out not to be his dream job. "The very thing that was cathartic for me was music," he says, "and all of a sudden it had this cloud of stress around it. So I started associating music with stress and deadlines and manufacturing plants messing up and bad reviews. It wasn't fun anymore." He talked a friend in Pittsburgh into taking the reins, so Misra moved out of Dayton, leaving Koe-Krompecher's Anyway Records as one of the few labels still active in the Buckeye State.

I asked DeLuca why such good music has manifested from the region, and he says isolation generates originality. "Ohio is a melting pot of the melting pot," he says. "It's not a very dualistic place. It's a swing state. It's a purple state. You can experience a lot of differ-ent cultures in Ohio, and it creates a well-rounded thing. As John Schmersal [of Brainiac] said, 'Ohio people are characteristically un-afraid of doing their own thing.' I agree."

# 5

## DAYTON

NICKNAMED THE GEM CITY, DAYTON IS THE HOMETOWN OF three *West Wing* cast members: Allison Janney, Martin Sheen, and Rob Lowe (though he moved to LA during his teen years). Comedian Dave Chappelle lives north of Dayton in Yellow Springs. Nowhere else in Ohio can claim those fun-filled celebrity facts. Yet the city also has some weird history with the Dayton Project aiding in the creation of the atomic bomb. Science aside, Dayton has always rocked hard. First, in the seventies and eighties, Dayton's funk culture exploded with the Ohio Players ("Love Rollercoaster"), Slave, and Sun. In the nineties, rock took over with Guided by Voices, Brainiac, and the Breeders comprising the trifecta of bands that gained national notoriety. Sure, there were a lot of other bands—Swearing at Motorists, Cage, Real Lulu, A Ten O'Clock Scholar—but those three shared the same bills, played Lollapalooza, and got the hell out of Dayton in a bigger way. Brainiac described Dayton—and its indie philosophy—best when they created T-shirts that read "Fuck y'all, we're from Dayton."

"I think it's a holdover from the days before everyone was so connected by the internet," says Tod Weidner, bassist in the Dayton group the Motel Beds, on why so many bands came up in Ohio, especially Dayton. "Before that, there was very much a make-your-own-fun mind-set. The Midwest was geographically and culturally isolated, so bands sprung up to fill the void. The world has changed, but the old tradition carried on, with bands filtering whatever they could use through a weird Midwestern filter and coupling it with this work ethic that people seem to have around here." Weidner grew up in the late eighties and nineties and has witnessed the culture adapting to modern times. "Bands nowadays have so much more competition for people's attention and leisure time," he says. "The main thing to do was to see bands play. You're trying to get kids to look up from their goddamn phones long enough to come to a show and engage."

Weidner thinks Dayton "tends to go through peaks and valleys" but also believes bands in Dayton are supportive of one another. "We're all friends with a lot of those folks. They're more peers than idols who we look up to. Having said that, I think they've all managed to carve out niches for themselves. Dayton's a pretty musical place, especially for the size town it is." The Motel Beds have been around since 2003 and have released a batch of albums, but they don't have grand ambitions to make it big. "We get together these days when the stars align, we record albums when we have enough songs to record an album, and we try to space out shows so that they're more of an event than just, 'Oh, the Beds are playing again,'" Weidner says. "It's a special occasion when we decide to do something now, which helps keep us happier than when we were bashing our heads against the wall, trying to get stuff going. None of us are under any illusion that a living can be made from music these days, given our situation. It's kind of freeing, really; we don't have to try to be anything in particular to anyone."

"You do find this mentality in Ohio that bands want to be the biggest one in their town," Jim Greer, former Guided by Voices bassist says. "They don't have ambitions beyond that. There are bands in Dayton that want to be big in Dayton. I understand people have day jobs and can't tour much, but if you have any ambitions other than playing out for your friends, you have to play other places."

Happy Chichester of Howlin' Maggie played Dayton's "Edgefest 96" and shared a stage with an Ohio legend. "I walked offstage and Bob Pollard gave me this nice compliment," he says. "When Guided by Voices got up, he praised our set, and we signed autographs and sold a thousand copies of the new record in Dayton that week. It's part of the reason I love Dayton. It's not only the bands that came out of there; it's the audiences and how true they are. They aren't just giving you lip service—they're buying your record and supporting you."

### BRAINIAC

*We were bringing together parts that had already existed and bringing them into the context for a band in the nineties coming from the Rust Belt.*

—John Schmersal

During the morning of May 23, 1997, Brainiac (stylized as 3RA-1N1AC) lead singer Tim Taylor drove his twenty-year-old vintage rusted Mercedes through the streets of Dayton. The vehicle was in such poor shape, it probably wouldn't have passed emissions testing. "He was going to try and sweet talk the cutie at the DMV [Department of Motor Vehicles] to see if he could get it to pass," his bandmate, guitarist John Schmersal, recalls Taylor telling him. "As foreshadowing as that moment was, Juan [Monasterio, bassist] and I laughed and got into the car and drove to Cincinnati. That was the last time I saw him." In Dayton the twenty-eight-year-old lost control of the car and slammed into two poles and a fire hydrant, causing his ride to explode. The cause of Taylor's death was carbon monoxide poisoning, which had built up in his system. "The toxicology report said he didn't have significant alcohol or drugs in his system," Schmersal says. "I thought he passed out from carbon monoxide and then died in the fire, but according to the autopsy, he was dead from carbon monoxide poisoning before that. It gives me a little peace that he didn't feel the crash or the burning. But I also find it a little hard to believe." Nine days before the accident, the band had played a show in England with Beck.

Taylor's untimely death came during a pivotal time in Brainiac's career. They had already released three full-lengths, two EPs, some singles, and were on the brink of signing to Interscope Records, after having been signed to the Chicago indie label Touch and Go. The week before Taylor's death, Schmersal had gotten into a car accident and totaled his car. Then his grandmother died the same weekend as Taylor. He was scheduled to fly to New York to possibly sign the record deal—he also had a wedding in North Carolina to attend—when the deaths occurred. "Suddenly I had no car and a good friend of mine, my bandmate, was gone. My grandmother was gone. I went to a wedding and two funerals," he says. Schmersal decided to spend the summer in New York to clear his head, which turned out to be good therapy for him. "It was an end of an era for me, but more so it was the beginning of a new thing for me as well," he says. "It was a good place to go to be distracted from the depression and the stuff I was dealing with."

Michelle Bodine, the band's original guitarist, found out about Tim's death through the news. "I was home, eating dinner, and the news was on," Bodine remembers. "I didn't totally pay attention for some reason, and I heard the policeman say it was the worst accident he'd ever seen. Then my cousin called me right after and told me. We gathered at his house that night, probably thirty people. Everyone was in total shock. What a terrible night." Three months after Taylor's death, the Breeders, Guided by Voices, Mink, and Swearing at Motorists played a benefit show in Dayton in honor of him.

Jim Greer, who had lived in Dayton and knew all of the bands, had just left town around the time Taylor died. The night he found out about Taylor's passing, he was staying with a friend in New York. "I got a call from Nils Bernstein, who was the publicist at Matador. He knew I was in town and called me at my friend's house at two in the morning and said, 'You have to come over here.' The weird thing is, Nils and I had been hanging out when Kurt Cobain shot himself. We can't be in the same town at the same time, because people die—that was a macabre joke we had between us. It was only three years after Kurt died when Timmy had his accident." Mired in a tragic coda, the four-piece experimental band disbanded, leaving behind a mythical legacy in the vein of Kurt Cobain and Nirvana. It left fans wondering: what if Timmy Taylor had not died? What if they would've signed to Interscope? Would they have maintained their cult following? Like Schmersal says, "Everything happened for a reason."

But let's rewind to the beginning. In March 1992, Brainiac—who were then called We'll Eat Anything—played their first gig, at Wright State University's cafeteria, with then members Taylor, drummer Tyler Trent, bassist Juan Monasterio, and the only female member, Bodine. (She would later join Heartless Bastards' Erika Wennerstrom in the Dayton group Shesus after forming the short-lived post-Brainiac band O-Matic with her brother.) Brainiac released their first record, *Smack Bunny Baby*, in 1993 on Grass Records. Schmersal was born in Toledo, lived in New Jersey for a while, and moved to Beavercreek (a Dayton 'burb) for the tenth grade, when he was fourteen years old. "There was a great underground music scene in Dayton when I got there," he says. He and Tyler Trent formed a band with fellow Dayton musician Jeremy Frederick named Sunken Giraffe, and they started playing gigs and attending shows at the Front Street warehouses. "[Promoter] Ken Gross—basically he's [responsible] for my DIY upbringing in Dayton," he says. "He brought out more important shows. It was a great environment for a city like Dayton, which wasn't considered a large hub in any way." Through these shows, Schmersal played with local punk group Haunting Souls—Tim Taylor lived with the group's singer, Jamy Holliday.

Schmersal left for Ohio University right when Brainiac formed. Bodine left the group in November 1993, and they needed a new guitarist. "Once they realized that they wanted to have a different guitar player, I was the first thing that came up. If I had put more time in school and not into playing music as an extracurricular activity, Tim and Juan wouldn't have been as aware of me as they were." At college,

Schmersal says, he wasn't "engaged." "I wanted to be there, but I was slowly realizing I was becoming disillusioned with whether or not I should continue at that point." The summer before Brainiac came along and changed his life, Schmersal was supposed to be saving money for school but instead spent his earnings on guitars and amps. "I've had these things a couple of times in my life where I'm like, is this a good idea or bad idea? I didn't have an intuition that I was going to be in a band, but I felt like I had to make these purchases. And six months later I was pretty much using all of them in Brainiac. It was one of things." When Taylor asked Schmersal to drop out of OU, move back to Dayton, and join the band, he was ready. "It was a no-brainer for me," he says. "They were already one of my favorite bands regionally, and they were from my former hometown. I quit at the end of that quarter and came in the winter [of 1994] to be in the band. I went to school there just long enough for what I needed mentally to accomplish."

Back in Dayton, rent was cheap; his share was sixty-seven dollars a month, but he had two roommates. "You can't beat rent that is that cheap," he jokes. "You can live at the poverty level and still pay your rent and go on tour. I worked at the record store Omega. I eventually moved to Cincinnati and was making burritos at the Comet. It was a fairly great lifestyle." *Bonsai Superstar* was the first record Schmersal played on, which was recorded in Brooklyn and produced by Girls Against Boys singer Eli Janney. (Pitchfork.com named it one of the best albums of the 1990s.[1])

The group toured the world and garnered the attention of Los Angelinos (and Brainiac obsessives) Griffin and Nathan Hamill— actor Mark Hamill's sons. Griffin, who is an artist and martial arts instructor, was thirteen when his brother (also an artist) introduced him to their music. "My brother had a tape deck in his car and had a copy of *Hissing Prigs in Static Couture*," Hamill says. "I remember being intrigued by the opening track, 'Indian Poker (Part 3).' But as soon as it segued into the next song, 'Pussyfootin',' I was apoplectic. That song was doing too much, and my brother had it blasting. I remember thinking how obnoxious it was—now I love it." (It's his favorite Brainiac record.) When the band played LA in June 1996, seventeen-year-old Nathan created a fan flyer for the show (fig. 27), and Griffin drew a picture of Brainiac for fun (fig. 28). "Brainiac definitely pushed boundaries but never in a nasty way," Hamill says.

> They were just thinking ahead, with a firm grasp of what came before them. Once John joined the band, I think they grew exponentially. They really listened to their contemporaries extremely well, because they used the spacing of the Breeders and Girls Against Boys and the visceral attack of Jesus Lizard and Shellac, and yet added so many more dimensions. They were James Brown meets Devo on acid, an utterly beguiling and dangerous concoction. Tim could deconstruct a pop song without getting in the way of its charm. He had a knack for finding humor in the abject.

Though they played shows on the coasts, they refrained from playing more than a few shows a year in Dayton. "Our thing was learning from the mistakes of what we called 'local band mentality,'" Schmersal says. "Most of the time local bands play too much locally and burn out their local audience instead of trying to strike out of their comfort zone and play shows out of town. We'd often do a hall show or pick a venue that didn't normally do shows and try to make it into a special, one-of-a-kind event."

It's hard to pinpoint Brainiac's sound, but Schmersal refers to it as "angular." When Schmersal first became a part of the group, Taylor tried to dissuade him from speaking his mind. "When I joined, there was something in that letter that Tim wrote to me that said, 'You won't have much creative input being the little Hitler that I am, but we'll have a lot of fun.' I was like, 'Whoa. How about that.' I didn't take that lying down. I was for presenting my ideas, and I think he quickly learned I had a lot more to offer than to just play the parts. I think he was annoyed with me at first, but then there were obviously useful things I brought to the table." Schmersal used pagers to make sounds, a tape delay effect called an Echoplex, and Moog synths. He also got into "hot-wiring a drum machine so it sounded like it was dying." "But I didn't think it was terribly unique," he says. "I can't imagine being in another band where I would be encouraged to play or record the sound of such a thing. That was the environment in Brainiac. Our approach, generally speaking, we didn't invent a new genre. We were bringing together parts that had already existed and bringing them into the context for a band in the nineties coming from the Rust Belt."

Akin to many other Ohio groups in the nineties that acquiesced to major label deals, Brainiac wasn't immune from it. "Back then, there were still tastemakers basically trying to figure out who these people were before they hit and who were taking a gamble on things," Schmersal says.

> There was a buzz on our band, but we were still a weird band and we struck out in a different market just like any other band. There was no internet and so people were still reading their local free press and looking at flyers and getting engaged about shows. There was much more of a DIY culture then than there is now. I think people are more engaged in festival culture these days. They save up their money to go to Coachella—that's what they splurge on for the year instead of seeing their favorite bands three times a month locally.

Schmersal considers Brainiac to be the third most popular band from Dayton during that time, next to the Breeders and Guided by Voices. "I didn't feel like calling New York a scene in the same way that being in Dayton was, because [Dayton] was smaller and therefore so much of a real scene," he says. "The network is finite. I thought more of the local scene being our band, because we were more DIY than those guys were." Brainiac, Guided by Voices, and the Breeders intermingled when they shared slots at Lollapalooza and when Kim Deal produced Brainiac's first Touch and Go release, the three-song *Internationale* EP, in 1995.

In March 1996 the group released *Hissing Prigs in Static Couture*, their last full-length record; the *Electro-Shock for President* EP came out a few weeks before Taylor's demise and was their final release. "When the band ended, I remember having a drink with a friend in a bar, and we were talking about what could have been," Schmersal says. "We were close to signing this major label deal. I'm into so much that isn't popular, so why should the music I make be any different than that? That's been my consolation." He's glad the group still resonates with fans and continues to make an impact. He explains that the reason is probably because of "our individuality—each [of the] four members of the band have their own unique character onstage and what they bring to the music. When [fans] saw us live, I wasn't sure what was going to happen. I didn't know how fast Tyler was going to play the song. There was a good part of unknown quotient to the performance. It was open for experimentation."

Griffin Hamill compares Brainiac's legacy to Joy Division, another group that released only a few records and whose lead singer died young. "Brainiac, in a strange way, is the same," Hamill says. "They were there for a short time but were utterly baffling, strange, and fun. They continue to inspire people because they are unique. Brainiac made a complete statement of intent and then enacted their plan. So many bands play it safe. Brainiac never did. They didn't take themselves too seriously, and they rocked with a smart-ass chaos. They are so personable on their records, and that's what comes through. They are the human in the machine."

A few years after Brainiac folded, Schmersal, who has a "soft spot for Dayton," formed the trio Enon (named after a Dayton exurb) with Skeleton Key member Rick Lee. Schmersal says he always wanted to work with Lee, and one day, while walking down the streets of New York, they crossed paths. "[Lee] said we should play together, and that's how that began." Enon released a few records but folded in 2011. Then in 2010 Schmersal moved to LA and joined the touring lineup of electronic group Caribou, manned by Dan Snaith. He now plays in the groups Vertical Scratchers and Crooks on Tape with Lee. Only once since 1997 have the remaining members of Brainiac played together, and that was in 2014 at a fund-raiser after the death of Jeremy Frederick. Bodine played with the band, and another Tim, Tim Krug, filled in on some parts. "It was seamless putting the set back together," Schmersal says.

Reflecting on his music career, Schmersal sees it was all linked. "I hear musicians talk about whether or not they feel lucky or if they were in the right place at the right time. But you can't continue to play music without putting some elbow grease into the situation. I went to college and I could have easily had never ended up in Brainiac, which led to all of these other things that I did. There's something to be said for following your heart and seeing where the opportunities are. I think about it a lot."

### THE BREEDERS

*Their music is a real joyful kind of thing.*

—Mike Montgomery

The thwumping bass line on the Top 40 hit "Cannonball" defined the mid-1990s post-grunge era and established the Breeders as MTV darlings. The 1993 platinum-selling *Last Splash* (4AD/Elektra Records) wasn't their first record—that would be 1990's *Pod*. Back then the Breeders lineup included Belly's Tanya Donelly and Kim Deal. Kim formed the Breeders as a subsidiary gig from her bass duties in the Pixies. However, in 1993 she was fresh from breaking up with the band and turned her full attention to the Breeders. In 1992 Kim's identical sister, Kelley, joined the band as guitarist (the first Breeders record she played on was the *Safari* EP, released soon after she joined the band), and Dayton-based Guided by Voices member (later with the Amps) Jim Macpherson enlisted his drums; the British Josephine Wiggs rounded up the lineup as bassist. Akin to Bob Pollard and Mitch Mitchell, the Deals grew up in North Dayton (Huber Heights). In 2012 I met and interviewed Kelley for the first time. I asked her why Dayton was such a weird place, but she couldn't pin down its essence.

"I do think Dayton is weird," she says.

> I think Dayton is kind of unique that for the size of the town we have [population less than two hundred thousand]; we've had some amazing bands come from there. I think there's something wonderful there and I don't know what it is. I know when Kim and I were growing up you played cover songs,

and as a girl you played keyboards and you played tambourine and sang. And that's all you did. The idea that Kim and I wrote original music—that's what was interesting to us. It was very unusual. A lot of towns have bands that are original, but it sure seems like we've had our fair share of good stuff.

Many people I talked to for this book are in accordance that the Breeders are one of the best bands to come out of Ohio—and from the rocksphere in general.

Happy Chichester says he "hears roots in Tommy James and the Shondells [James was born in Dayton; the Michigan-based band is known for "Crimson and Clover" and "Hanky Panky"] giving way to this melodic, poppy Ohio Express bubblegum," he says. "It's not like they were doing teeny-bop bubblegum fare, but the simple elegance of these melodies and chord constructions, they still persist these days and it puts a smile on my face when I hear that. That's the great thing about Ohio: there's these echoes and roots that are strong."

Heartless Bastards front woman Erika Wennerstrom grew up in Dayton and was aware of the Deals. "When I was in high school, the Breeders' 'Cannonball' was number one on the radio," she says. "I think that gave me a lot of inspiration, because the Breeders are from Dayton, and seeing a band do that well and in alternative music—they weren't mainstream pop—it really gave me a lot of hope and it made me feel like I didn't need to leave Ohio to find success, either." Wennerstrom has played with Kelley Deal in a couple of incarnations. First, Kelley's band R. Ring opened for the Bastards at the old Southgate House in Cincinnati in 2011; Wennerstrom also played a solo show with Kelley in Dayton in 2016. "She's just such an amazing and warm person," she says about Kelley. "It's always nice when you meet some of your inspirations and heroes and you see they're truly good people. I think she's truly kind."

Kelley's cohort in R. Ring, Mike Montgomery, wasn't too familiar with the Breeders' discography when he and Deal joined forces in 2011. He says he knew of "Cannonball," but when he'd go to the record store, he only had so much money to spend and that money would go to bands like Sonic Youth and the Dead Kennedys. "I didn't get into their whole catalog until I started playing with Kelley, and I wanted to see what other shit she had done. I wanted to dig into her past a little bit." In 2013 the Deals tapped him to be their roadie on the twentieth-anniversary *Last Splash* world tour. So Montgomery acquainted himself with their style. "Did they influence me in my formative years? No," he says, "But did they influence me once I dug in, and do they continue to influence me? Yes, they do. But I wish I would have gotten into them twenty years ago."

During the tour, he made some conspicuous observations about the sisters. "It's easy for me to forget, sometimes, that really they mean a whole bunch to a lot of people—and deservedly," he says.

There's a casualness to the way their music comes across, even in the way they would set up for a show. We might be playing some giant festival with all this crew and then the Breeders set up their gear that we dragged out of Kim's basement. They throw it onstage and play a great set of timeless songs. I was never not impressed with the lack of fluff and fanfare with which they present themselves and the songs, because I think one thing that's different from the Breeders and a lot of other bands is, at the core the Breeders are a song-based band, meaning that the songs stand on their own. So they can go and do a show and play great song after great song after great song. They don't need extra trappings of big production, like lights and fog, because they're focused on the songs. Every song comes across as super easy and breezy and has a fun looseness to it. But I didn't realize, until I started working with them and got inside of it, that every little nuance is extremely thought out and pored over and groomed and caressed and nurtured and intentional. That impressed me more about the band: how intentional every little inch was on the record. But it sounds so easy when you're listening to it.

Kelley Deal brings that "casualness" to R. Ring shows, too. Seeing them is an intimate experience in which the audience is invited to interact with Deal and Montgomery.

Philip Kim's band Connections opened for the Breeders once and had a thought process similar to that of Montgomery. "They don't seem greedy," he says.

They don't seem like they're trying to make a ton of music or be the biggest band of the world. That's something I look for in music. I just love their song-writing in general. It does have a certain Midwest quality. I don't know how to describe Midwest quality, though. It may seem their songs are minimal and simple, but it actually requires a lot of expertise and talent and work to make them really great songs. It sounds easy for them—same with Guided by Voices—very short songs, minimal-ish. But they are really great pop songs with great melodies, and they're masterful at songwriting and playing their instruments. That's key as well. I think all the Breeders are top-notch musicians.

"I think they've been role models to me just in terms of women doing their own thing," Annie Zaleski says. "They go their own path and don't necessarily buy into or care about what's cool." (There's a reason why the Dandy Warhols wrote a song called "Cool as Kim Deal.")

And what Griffin Hamill loves best about the Breeders is how limited their musical skills are. "I like those limitations," he says. "They just sound like a real band, like Brainiac was. They make [music] for themselves and are pretty experimental for a pop group. I love the textures they create and how organic their music sounds."

In my experiences with Kelley (I have not met Kim), I think she's warm and unpretentious. When I met her, I thought to myself, *This woman toured the world with Nirvana. She's a rock star.* But she's one of the most down-to-earth people I've ever met. In 2012 R. Ring opened for the band Low in Cincinnati. During Low's performance, Kelley sat in the corner of the Taft Theatre and knitted. I don't think anyone else noticed Kelley's insouciant behavior during the concert. I thought, *Now, that's rock and roll.*

After *Last Splash* the Breeders released more albums and EPs, but sporadically. *Title TK* came out in 2002, *Mountain Battles* was released in 2008, and then came the 2009 EP *Fate to Fatal.* The Breeders are still, thankfully, active (in 2017 they embarked on a fall tour), but Kelley's other focus is R. Ring, that released their debut full-length, *Ignite the Rest* (on Dayton, Kentucky's SofaBurn Records), in 2017. The setup is just Kelley on guitar, Mike on bass, and rotating touring drummers. Their songs waver between stripped-down lush melodies and harder rock. Before they released the album, they released a series of singles. At first Kelley and Mike were against releasing a twelve-song record, though. "We never wanted to necessarily have the pressure of going into a studio and sitting down and banging out a full-length record, and then over time, all of a sudden, we just had a bunch of songs," Montgomery says. "We're like, maybe it'd be nice. It'd be good way to put a period at the end of this six-year-long sentence. We didn't want to have any guidelines or timelines. If we wanted to go and play shows, we wanted to go and play."

The Breeders signify so many things—a women-fronted rock band that made it out of Dayton; great pop-music songwriters; talent to heighten simple songs into something more complex—but the biggest attribute is bliss. "Their music is a real joyful kind of thing," Montgomery says. "I know they're real proud to be from Dayton, and they've got some West Virginia Appalachian roots, and they're real proud of that, too. There's no sense of them playing to the establishment—they're just doing their thing, unashamedly, and their thing just happens to be real good."

### GUIDED BY VOICES

*We're the* Pinocchio *story: we became a real boy.*

—Bob Pollard

In April 2017 Bob Pollard touched a capstone. The Guided by Voices (GBV) double album *August by Cake* became his one-hundredth release in his entire oeuvre, which includes more than twenty-four full-length GBV albums, side projects, and solo stuff, dating back to 1983 when he started the band in his North Dayton basement. Since then, Pollard has drafted more than fifty different musicians to play in the band (mostly all white males), in a prime example of the term "rotating lineup." Jeff Warren painstakingly catalogs everything GBV—set lists, photos, discography lists—on the online Guided by Voices Database (GBVDB.com).[2] Here's what I learned: GBV has played the most shows in New York City, followed by Chicago, and then Dayton. Between 2000 and 2004 they averaged sixty shows a year. "It's a full-time job keeping up with what Bob puts out," says Jim Greer, former GBV bass player and author of the biography *Guided by Voices: A Brief History: Twenty-One Years of Hunting Acci-*

*dents in the Forests of Rock and Roll.*[3] Greer dedicates forty-five pages of his book alone to GBV releases and thirty-four pages to Pollard's adjacent projects. Needless to say, Pollard is prolific.

Greer attributes Pollard's productivity to his blue-collar upbringing. "He's never had writer's block," Greer says. ("Writer's block is for pussies," Pollard says in Greer's book.) "He gets up in the morning and puts on a pot of coffee and writes songs. That's what he does. It's the discipline of a former schoolteacher—he considers it his job. For every song that he does put out, though, there's two or three he doesn't even record, because he writes three times as many songs as he puts out. He has an amazing brain and a wild imagination and a gift for melody. Honestly, you can have all that stuff and still not produce the way he does."

To get a better idea of Pollard's inexhaustible mind, I ask him how's he able to do it. "Well, first of all, I've absorbed a lot of good rock," he says.

> My formative years were during the golden era of rock ('66 to '79), and I'm still inspired by music from that period. I stay prolific because I never really take a break. Writing songs and making collages is an intermingled, ongoing process. It's all I do, and it's really all I can do well. I don't force anything. Occasionally I become inspired, and that's when I storm songs onto a cassette tape. I fill notebooks with lyrical ideas and go from there. Then we record, put out a record, and take it on the road. The road can be exhausting, but it's a blast playing shows.

It's helpful that most of Pollard's tunes are terse, clocking in at less than three minutes.

Pollard taught fourth grade while clamoring away in his home, writing songs and recording them on a four-track recorder. It wasn't until the late eighties, but more so the mid-nineties when he decided to let the rest of the world hear his music. Greer moved to Dayton from New York in 1991 because his then girlfriend, Kim Deal, wanted to move back home. He was a senior editor for *Spin* magazine and infiltrated the so-called Dayton music scene, writing about local bands for the publication. Even though Greer lived in town and thought he knew everyone in the music sphere, it took his visiting the Matador Records office in New York to discover GBV. An employee handed Greer a seven-inch record, *The Grand Hour*, featuring the song "Shocker in Gloomtown." The guy said, "'This is probably the best thing we're distributing right now,' and I looked at the address: Dayton, Ohio? I live in Dayton, Ohio. How have I not heard of these guys?'" When Greer returned to Dayton, he phoned up Pollard and the two started hanging out. "They were older than the other bands and hadn't played out for seven years, at that time," Greer says. "They had been forgotten." That is, until the Breeders covered "Shocker in Gloomtown" on their 1994 *Head to Toe* EP and Deal hyped them up in interviews. That led to the *New York Times'* wanting to do a story on the "Dayton scene." "They called and asked if I'd do a scene report on Dayton," Greer says. "I had to explain to them there was no scene in Dayton, not one that deserved a national profile. One of the reasons was because there was a lack of places to play, and [the] Breeders, Brainiac, and Guided by Voices were the only bands that played outside of Dayton."

Pollard agrees. "It was really good in the nineties with the Breeders, Brainiac, Swearing at Motorists, us, and a few others," he says, "but there wasn't really a scene. There weren't really many places to play or even hang out." The Canal Street Tavern's small space challenged bands, but there was a semblance of a scene at the bar Walnut Hills, near the University of Dayton. "Between 1992 and 1996 there was some sort of community, just because everybody was hanging out and drinking at the same bar. We had our own booth at Walnut Hills," Greer says.

In 1995 Pollard asked Greer to join the band as bassist; he played on 1995's *Alien Lanes*, one of their most revered records. "In the nineties in Guided by Voices, we didn't make any money," Greer says. "We made a little bit of money, maybe enough that you could almost live on in Dayton, which is the cheapest place in the world. And we were unusually successful at that time." At first it was only supposed to be a part-time gig for him, but it quickly turned into a career. "It turned into a full-time job and that's ultimately why I had to quit,"

Greer says. "It got to be too much for me. I have an issue of occasional panic attacks onstage. Now I don't have that anymore, so it's fine. But back then I didn't know what was happening. I was freaking out and then self-medicating with alcohol. It had to stop. And I had to get out of Dayton, and I did [in 1997 he moved to LA]. I love Bob and we're still good friends, and I loved playing in his band, but I couldn't keep doing it." He explains that Pollard isn't the easiest person to work with. "In the band, it's always been Bob's way or the highway. Bob is very mercurial. It's cliché, but it's accurate. He'll just decide for what seems like no logical reason to fire everybody, even if it's in the middle of a tour. But it's logical to him."

Like in *The Godfather*, Greer tried to flee the clan, but Pollard pulled him back in. In the fall of 2004 Pollard called Greer and said, "'It's time.' I said, 'Time for what?' Apparently when I was in the band, we had discussed that when the band broke up I would write a biography on them. I did not remember that, but I was happy to do it." GBV played two send-off shows on New Year's Eve 2004 at Chicago's Metro concert hall. Greer had only two months to write the book, including covering the final performances; the book came out in 2005. Pollard spent the next five years releasing solo works and other projects. In 2010 former label Matador asked Pollard to reunite the 1993–1996 iteration, the "classic lineup"—Mitch Mitchell, Tobin Sprout, Greg Demos, Kevin Fennell—for a twenty-first-anniversary party in Vegas for the label. Pollard thought, *Well, if they do a reunion show, they might as well do a full tour and then release more records*—which is what occurred. Fans had concocted the term "classic lineup" (Pollard didn't like the name), which never existed on any record. "'The classic lineup' was seen by almost no one and didn't exist as a single unit," Greer says. "You can't override what's in the public imagination. It doesn't matter; what matters is people's perception of it."

After Greer left Dayton in 1997, he embarked on a career as a novelist and a screenplay writer. He formed the band DTCV (pronounced "Detective") and played a show with Guided by Voices in

Dayton in 2016. "Whenever I see Bob, it's a massive drinking session," he says. "I have to steel myself to prepare for it. It's hard to keep up." DTCV played a show in Cincinnati as part of MidPoint Music Festival 2013, and Pollard came to see them play. "After the show, we stayed at the bar until they kicked us out," Greer says. "Bob was buying shot after shot of tequila. When you hang out with him, that's what happens. It was a blast, but if I had to do that every single night, I'd be dead."

Yes, maybe Pollard is a "functional alcoholic," but he rarely forgets lyrics during his live shows, which sometimes last three hours. "The impressive part to me—this is part of one of his secrets—is he doesn't forget the lyrics to all of those songs, no matter how drunk he gets," Greer says. "In fact, the drunker he gets, the better his memory gets sometimes. Having said that, he does sometimes forget the words, but it doesn't matter, because he'll make up different words, and people won't notice. Or he'll rearrange the verses. He does screw up occasionally but it's so rare. That makes it all the more exceptional. He just has a brain that remembers."

A hundred and one records in—GBV released *How Do You Spell Heaven* in August 2017—and Pollard probably hasn't gotten his due. *Bee Thousand* (GBV's 1994 breakout record, distributed by Scat) and *Alien Lanes* (their eighth studio album) are considered two of the greatest records of the 1990s, so much so that Delaware brewery Dogfish Head released a beer named Beer Thousand in 2014. Greer thinks part of the reason why he hasn't garnered enough deference is that a lot of GBV fanatics are too focused on his earlier lo-fi material, before Pollard adapted to a higher-quality studio.

"He's put out some great records that haven't gotten the recognition [they deserve]," he says. "In the fullness of time, they will. When they were reunited, they were bigger than they had been before. People tend to take things for granted. When they went away, they influenced other bands, like the Strokes."

"We're the *Pinocchio* story: we became a real boy," Pollard says about GBV's legacy. "We stuck to our guns and were rewarded with acceptance, a hard-core following, a record contract, and respect. It's inspirational not only to Dayton bands and Ohio bands, but bands everywhere. I didn't get to make it a career until I was thirty-six years old. That gives hope and a reason to persevere to a lot of young people who want to make records and play rock and roll. But I think the legacy, beyond that, will be the sheer amount of songs, and depending on who you talk to, good songs, in the catalog."

Bob Pollard's favorite Ohio bands:

**The Ohio Express:** 1960s pop band from Mansfield known for "Yummy Yummy Yummy."

**The James Gang:** '60s/'70s rock band from Cleveland known for "Funk #45."

**Pere Ubu:** Weird art-rockers from Cleveland formed by Peter Laughner and David Thomas

**The Raspberries:** Top 40 power-pop group from Cleveland influenced by British Invasion bands

**The Electric Eels:** '70s punk band from Cleveland that played only five shows

**The Mirrors:** '70s punk band from Cleveland that released only a few songs

**The Styrenes:** '70s punk band from Cleveland with members of Electric Eels and the Mirrors

**Thomas Jefferson Slave Apartments:** '90s lo-fi band from Columbus featuring Ron House of Great Plains

**The Mice:** '80s power-pop group from Cleveland

**Death of Samantha:** '80s post-punk band from Cleveland, with some members playing in GBV

**The Breeders:** Popular '90s pop-rock band from Dayton featuring the Deal sisters

**Vertical Slit:** '70s/'80s lo-fi rock band from Columbus's Jim Shepard

"And, oh, yes, my favorite by far is Devo, especially the early, scary-ass Devo," Pollard says.

## THE TERRIFYING EXPERIENCE

*We were at a party and we were playing with a Ouija board, and
we said, "Should we start a band?" And it said, "Yes."*

—Mitch Mitchell

It's early January and the temperature outside is a balmy ten degrees—and sinking. I am gathered with Dayton trio ("The Triumvirate") the Terrifying Experience, at Therapy Cafe in downtown
Dayton to see them in a double-bill show. Not only is it freezing
outside, but it's also frigid inside. Thankfully, the band has come to
turn up the heat and "to bring back rock and roll." Keeping my puffy
jacket on for warmth, I huddle on a couch with some Dayton relics,
tattooed musicians Mitch Mitchell, Luis Lerma, and his wife, Erin
Lerma (El Beano), who comprise two of the three bands playing
tonight: Terrifying Experience (TEX) and Team Void. On and off
since 1983, Mitchell has played in Guided by Voices—most notably
the "classic lineup" and the 2010–2014 reunion—but lately he hasn't
been involved at all. "I don't know what happened with that," he says.
"It was going on for a while and it kind of stopped. I didn't press the
issue." He and front man Bob Pollard have known each other since
childhood, when they played in a metal cover band called Anacrusis, in their home base of North Dayton. Lerma didn't grow up in
Dayton—he spent time in Texas and Portugal before settling in Dayton in the seventies. He, like Mitchell, has been playing in various
Dayton-based bands for decades. He was a member of the Tasties
and in 1995 played bass for Kim Deal's group the Amps, which released one album, *Pacer*, while the Breeders were on pause. "I got to
tour all over the world, and I got to meet all of my heroes, who turned
out to be my peers," Lerma says about the band. "It helped me out as
far as what we're doing right now." El Beano grew up in the Dayton
suburb of Centerville (where I grew up!) and always liked to sing,
and she eventually learned to play guitar and bass.

I ask the three of them why so many bands form in Ohio, and Luis
and Mitch agree it's because of boredom. "There's not a whole lot to

do, so you get together with your buddies and make noise and have some drinks and go from there," Mitchell says. "A lot of guys never make it out of Dayton. They play here and never tour. Other bands get lucky." Luis adds why he believes bands don't leave Dayton: "It's because they get caught up on something they're not. You have to have a commitment to yourself to explore yourself and your community, and then hopefully find something that represents yourself and your community."

GBV were among the fortunates who escaped the dregs of their hometown. "First we had no success and then we got lucky," Mitchell says. "Somebody played a cassette tape at a party and somebody happened to hear it and it happened to be a label person. Getting signed opened up a lot of doors for us. But originally we did it for our own enjoyment." Long before Mitchell joined Anacrusis and then GBV, he tapped Kevin Fennell (who would later play in GBV) and Scott Bianco to play in Blue Mist/Ambush. "We liked music and decided we were going to have a band," Mitchell says. "I learned how to play the bass. Kevin played the drums, and Scott played guitar. We were eleven years old when we started playing."

In 1997 Mitchell founded the group TEX as a means to have his own band outside of GBV. "I always wanted to write songs and record it myself just for fun," he says. "I didn't write songs in GBV, because you had Tobin [Sprout] and Bob, and I wasn't going to try to get in on that. There was no reason for me to do that, so I just did it for myself." Over the years, TEX released two full-length albums, an EP, and some singles. However, the current incarnation of TEX evolved in 2016 when Mitchell recruited Lerma and El Beano to play. "We were at a party and we were playing with a Ouija board and we said, 'Should we start a band?' And it said, 'Yes,'" Mitchell says. El Beano and Luis's band, Team Void, needed a drummer, so Mitchell volunteered his services. Adding to the "triumvirate," all three of them know how to play bass guitar. "We're going to have a bass throwdown," Mitchell jokes.

Why is Dayton's music so weird? "You have the bodies of the aliens at Hanger 18 that radiate a weird energy," Mitchell theorizes. "It's conducive to rock musicians. A lot of weirdos come from here." (Hanger 18 is the mythical section at Wright-Patterson Air Force Base where it is rumored that corpses from a crashed UFO are stored. Yeah, like I keep saying, Dayton is an odd place.) "You have the biggest amount of inventors, writers, and poets here," Luis says—for instance, the Wright Brothers, humorist Erma Bombeck, and poet Paul Laurence Dunbar. The main creative force driving the Dayton scene has always been rock and roll, starting with funk bands to heavier-sounding ones. "Back in the day, one night you could see a funk band at the Lakeview Palladium and the next night go to Hara Arena and see Judas Priest," Mitchell says. Lerma thinks the current Dayton scene has become more independent than it used to be. "You don't have to listen to the status quo and you can be whomever you want," he says, "and hopefully you'll get people to tag in on it. Back then, when we started out, there were only a few venues, and we used to get spat on and get cursed at for writing original hard-core music. It's been a real struggle. It's the ones who are committed that make a success."

Although Mitchell is one of the most successful musicians to hail from Dayton, he has concurrently rocked and rolled and managed a trucking company for more than two decades. "The rock thing is something I've done my whole life and will always do it," he says. "I've had opportunities that a lot of people only dream about. If I can get lucky again and have success with it, I'll be super happy. But if not, and if we do what we're doing now, I'll still be just as happy. Music—I love it so much. I couldn't live without it."

Our interview concludes right before Daytonian Nicky Kay—who is a good friend of Mitchell's—starts things off with his instrumental orchestra; he gets bonus points for integrating a Theremin (an instrument played using electronic waves but no physical contact) into the set. About fifty concertgoers, who gather near the stage, create enough body heat to warm up the joint. Next up is

TEX, whose three members wear matching long-sleeve red, white, and black T-shirts with a "3" centered on them to symbolize the triumvirate. Mitchell wears a leather Motörhead vest, and they all wear biker hats. Mitchell shouts to the audience, "This is a rock and roll show. Hopefully this show will fuckin' rock." And it does. They barrel through their noisy rock tunes, and at one point Mitchell jokingly asks Lerma what he's rebelling against: "Whaddya, got?" Lerma says, imitating Marlon Brando in *The Wild One*. Watching them is similar to seeing your friend's band play. It feels hyper local; it feels good. "Rock and roll will kill us. I can't think of a better way to die," Mitchell says between songs.

After playing for about thirty minutes, they take a brief break and mask up for Team Void. They've switched positions now: Mitchell moves from guitar to drums, Lerma exchanges drums for guitar, and El Beano continues to play bass. Her mask is ninja-like, Lerma's is a skull, and Mitchell wears more of a traditional *luchador* wrestling mask. At this point most of the earlier crowd has dissipated. It's almost 1:00 a.m., and the temperature continues to drop. In our conversation, Mitchell mentioned something about rock and roll being cold-blooded. I finally understand what he meant—both its literal and figurative meaning (but mostly literal—it's cold!). As Team Void jams an instrumental-only set of warm surf-rock-inspired songs, I think to myself, *This is what unadulterated rock looks and sounds like*. TEX's goal was to bring back rock and roll—however brief—and during the bitterly cold night, they have resurrected it from the dead.

A few months after this night, the Lermas departed TEX, leaving Mitchell to replace them with new musicians. (Team Void lives on but without Mitchell on the skins.) Luis says, "We had to stop it just like we started it—quickly and professionally," and adds that the band "did not come together for us." At least we'll always have the memory of that rock and roll night.

# Notes

## 1. Akron/Kent

1. Robert Christgau, "A Real New Wave Rolls Out of Ohio," *Village Voice*, April 17, 1978, https://www.robertchristgau.com/xg/rock/ohio-78.php.

2. *It's Everything, and Then It's Gone*, directed by Phil Hoffman, 2003, Western Reserve Public Media/PBS; *If You're Not Dead, Play*, directed by Phil Hoffman, 2005, Western Reserve Public Media/PBS.

3. Jade Dellinger and David Giffels, *We Are DEVO!* (London: SAF Publishing, 2003); David Giffels, *The Hard Way on Purpose: Essays and Dispatches from the Rust Belt* (New York: Scribner, 2014).

4. LeBron James, "I'm Coming Home," *Sports Illustrated*, July 11, 2014, www .si.com/nba/2014/07/11/lebron-james-cleveland-cavaliers.

5. Susan Schmidt Horning, *Chasing Sound: Technology, Culture, and the Art of Studio Recording from Edison to the LP* (Baltimore: Johns Hopkins University Press, 2013).

6. Dellinger and Giffels, *We Are DEVO!*

7. Chrissie Hynde, *Reckless: My Life as a Pretender* (New York: Doubleday, 2015).

## 2. Cincinnati

1. Randy McNutt, *The Cincinnati Sound* (Mount Pleasant, SC: Arcadia Publishing, 2007).

2. Michaelangelo Matos and Stacey Anderson, "The Best Record Stores in the USA," RollingStone.com, September 16, 2010.

### 3. Cleveland

1. Brian Dulik, "Josh Cribs Voices Frustration after Another Defeat," *The Chronicle*, November 28, 2011, www.chroniclet.com/browns-notes/2011/11/28 /Josh-Cribbs-voices-frustration-after-another-defeat.html.

2. Joyce Halasa, "Great Scott!," *Scene*, November 2, 1989.

3. Dave Richards, *SHOWcase*, May 11, 1989.

4. "Jane Scott: Too Old for Rock and Roll," *Rolling Stone*, May 17, 1979.

5. Gregory Stricharchuk, "Jane Scott Knows Her Rock and Roll, Even If She Is 67," *Wall Street Journal*, March 24, 1987, 1.

6. Paul Singer, "Rock of Ages: A Venerable Music Critic Retires," Associated Press, May 6, 2002.

7. Jane Scott, "Jane Scott, Witness to Rock History: From the Beatles to Hip-Hop—a Personal Farewell," *Plain Dealer*, April 12, 2002.

8. Troy L. Smith, "101 Most Important songs in Cleveland Music History," *Cleveland.com*. March 22, 2017, www.cleveland.com/entertainment/index .ssf/2017/03/101_most_important_songs_in_cl.html.

### 4. Columbus

1. Ethan Smith and Mike Flaherty, "Columbus, Ohio: Local Heroes," *Entertainment Weekly*, March 17, 1995, 28–30.

2. Andy Downing and Joel Oliphint, "Little Brother's, Big Shoes," Columbus Alive, June 28, 2017, www.columbusalive.com/entertainment/20170628 /little-brothers-big-shoes.

3. Bela Koe-Krompecher, "Ohio," *Belakoekrompecher's Blog*, June 21, 2016, bela koekrompecher.wordpress.com/2016/06/21/ohio-repost-from-2010-for-cleveland.

4. Eric Davidson, *We Never Learn: The Gunk Punk Undergut, 1998–2001* (New York: Backbeat Books, 2010).

### 5. Dayton

1. Pitchfork Staff, "Top 100 Albums of the 1990s," Pitchfork.com, November 17, 2003, pitchfork.com/features/lists-and-guides/5923-top-100-albums-of-the-1990s.

2. Jeff Warren, Guided by Voices Database, gbvdb.com/cities.asp.

3. James Greer, *Guided by Voices: A Brief History: Twenty-One Years of Hunting Accidents in the Forests of Rock and Roll* (New York: Grove Press, 2005).

# Selected Bibliography

Christgau, Robert. "A Real New Wave Rolls Out of Ohio." *Village Voice*. April 17, 1978. https://www.robertchristgau.com/xg/rock/ohio-78.php.

Dellinger, Jade, and David Giffels. *We Are Devo!* London: SAF Publishing, 2003.

Davidson, Eric. *We Never Learn: The Gunk Punk Undergut, 1988–2001*. New York: Backbeat Books, 2010.

Downing, Andy, and Joel Oliphint. "Little Brother's, Big Shoes." Columbus Alive. June 28, 2017. www.columbusalive.com/entertainment/20170628/little-brothers-big-shoes.

Dulik, Brian. "Josh Cribs Voices Frustration after Another Defeat." *The Chronicle*. November 28, 2011. www.chroniclet.com/browns-notes/2011/11/28/Josh-Cribbs-voices-frustration-after-another-defeat.html.

Giffels, David. *The Hard Way on Purpose: Essays and Dispatches from the Rust Belt*. New York: Scribner, 2014.

Greer, James. *Guided by Voices: A Brief History: Twenty-One Years of Hunting Accidents in the Forests of Rock and Roll*. New York: Grove Press, 2005.

——— . "We're with the Band." *Spin*. May 2010.

Halasa, Joyce. "Great Scott!" *Scene*. November 2, 1989.

Horning, Susan Schmidt. *Chasing Sound: Technology, Culture, and the Art of Studio Recording from Edison to the LP*. Baltimore: Johns Hopkins University Press, 2013.

Hynde, Chrissie. *Reckless: My Life as a Pretender*. New York: Doubleday, 2015.

James, LeBron. "I'm Coming Home." *Sports Illustrated*. July 11, 2014. www.si.com/nba/2014/07/11/lebron-james-cleveland-cavaliers.

"Jane Scott: Too Old for Rock and Roll." *Rolling Stone*. May 17, 1979.

Koe-Krompecher, Bela. "Ohio." *Belakoekrompecher's Blog.* June 21, 2016. belakoek
   rompecher.wordpress.com/2016/06/21/ohio-repost-from-2010-for-cleveland.
Matos, Michaelangelo, and Stacey Anderson. "The Best Record Stores in the USA."
   RollingStone.com. September 16, 2010.
McNutt, Randy. *The Cincinnati Sound.* Mount Pleasant, SC: Arcadia Publishing,
   2007.
Pitchfork Staff. "Top 100 Albums of the 1990s." Pitchfork.com. November 17, 2003.
   pitchfork.com/features/lists-and-guides/5923-top-100-albums-of-the-1990s.
Richards, Dave. *SHOWcase*, May 11, 1989.
Scott, Jane. "Jane Scott, Witness to Rock History: From the Beatles to Hip-Hop—a
   Personal Farewell." *Plain Dealer.* April 12, 2002.
Singer, Paul. "Rock of Ages: A Venerable Music Critic Retires." Associated Press.
   May 6, 2002.
Smith, Ethan, and Mike Flaherty. "Columbus, Ohio: Local Heroes." *Entertainment
   Weekly.* March 17, 1995.
Smith, Troy L. "101 Most Important songs in Cleveland Music History."
   *Cleveland.com.* March 22, 2017. www.cleveland.com/entertainment/index
   .ssf/2017/03/101_most_important_songs_in_cl.html.
Stricharchuk, Gregory. "Jane Scott Knows Her Rock and Roll, Even If She Is 67."
   *Wall Street Journal.* March 24, 1987.
Warren, Jeff. Guided by Voices Database. gbvdb.com/cities.asp.

*Note: Most of this book's content was created from phone, email, and in-person
   interviews conducted between December 2016 and April 2017 and retained in
   the author's archives.*

**Garin Pirnia** was born and raised in the rock and roll city of Dayton, Ohio. She moved to the even more rock city of Los Angeles and then to Chicago, where she cut her teeth writing about music. She lives in Covington, Kentucky, with her cat, Diablo, and boyfriend, Adam. Since 2004, she has written about music (and film, food, TV, art) for *Rolling Stone, Vanity Fair, Mental Floss*, the *Wall Street Journal, The Atlantic, Paste* magazine, and many more publications. She is the author of *The Beer Cheese Book*, a cookbook/culinary tour of Kentucky. When she's not interviewing rock stars (or eating beer cheese), Garin is also an accomplished screenwriter. *The Finicky Cat*, a short horror comedy, has won several awards at film fests and screenplay contests. Music, beer cheese, and cats— she does it all.